This practical, faith-building guide
addresses:

- Divorce: living with a new reality
- Loneliness: removing your fear
- Despair: finding new hope for
  tomorrow
- Guilt: how to find peace
- Forgiveness: using an ancient
  remedy for inner healing
- Giving thanks: tapping the myste-
  rious power of thankfulness

"To live is to meet with adversity.
Some days we face only minor irritations.
Other times, it's a test of strength that
challenges our faith and endurance to
the limit." Instead of losing hope in the
face of trials and tragedies, learn to
view them as opportunities to exercise
your faith. Discover *How to Bend
Without Breaking*.

Larry Jones, the author of several
inspirational books, is a TV evangelist
whose program is aired on 100 stations
throughout the U.S. Larry Jones Inter-
national Ministries operates the world
hunger-relief organization "Feed the
Children."

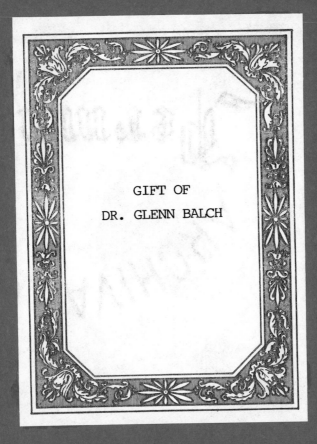

HOW TO
BEND
WITHOUT
BREAKING

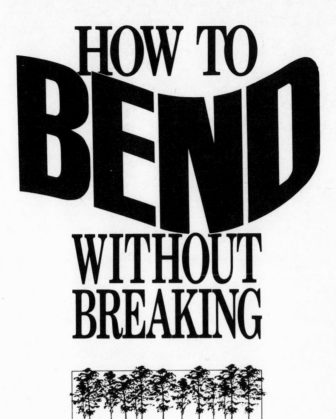

BY Larry Jones

How to Make It to Friday

Practice to Win

Feed the Children

How to Bend Without Breaking

HOW TO
BEND
WITHOUT
BREAKING

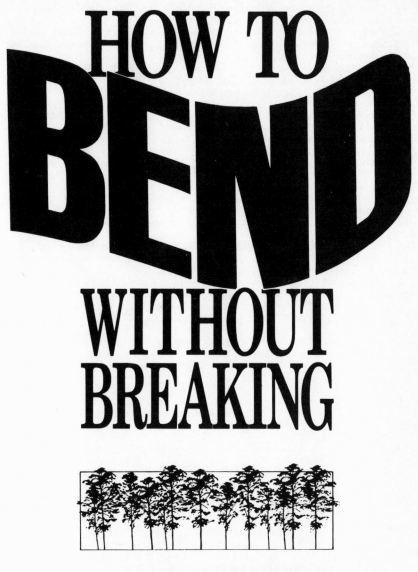

LARRY JONES

Fleming H. Revell Company
Old Tappan, New Jersey

CONTENTS

PART III

Attitude Adjustments:
Improving the conditions that hinder
healthy growth

Preface

In some ways, I've been writing this book all my life. Only in the last few years, however, has the concept begun to surface more strongly, each time I confronted a crisis in my life or watched others react to tragedies in their own.

I am convinced that the strength and quality of life is rooted in the ability to develop and maintain an attitude that allows one to *bend and not break* inside—no matter what's happening on the outside. That is what this book is all about.

This is not a book of easy answers. There are no simple solutions to life's most difficult problems; at least, if there are, I haven't discovered them. This book addresses the hard questions we all face at one time or another. Life isn't fair; it never will be. Good people are victimized by the acts of thoughtless, uncaring—yes, even evil people. Hardworking, unselfish men and women are forced from their land, uprooted in the sunset of their lives.

Why is it that some people are able to withstand the winds of misfortune and catastrophe while others simply fall apart and break under the stress? Why do some become bitter and defeated while others emerge victorious—scarred and bruised, but conquerors just the same?

Even in my own life, I've experienced times when I was able to bounce back from adversity with speed and clarity. Yet, why couldn't I do the same thing when a series of events threatened the future of my ministry?

As I explored these questions, I kept returning to the analogy of the tree. When the storm winds blow, the tree bends low to the ground. If its roots are deep and its branches are healthy, the tree can withstand the force of the storm. It will *bend but not break*. When the storm subsides, the tree returns to its upright position. That's why I've included lessons from the trees after each chapter. For me, they've been a tremendous source of information and encouragement because nature's healing powers are marvelous wonders, and we're all a part of God's wondrous creation.

To live is to meet with adversity. Some days we face only minor irritations. Other times, it's a test of strength that challenges our faith and endurance to the limit. Only in death are we freed of problems—and that's not an attractive alternative. Despite its problems, life is *good*.

I like the words of Robert Browning's poem "The Common Problem":

> *The common problem, yours, mine, everyone's,*
> *Is—not to fancy what were fair in life*
> *Provided it could be—but, finding first*
> *What may be, then find how to make it fair*
> *Up to our means.*

As the Apostle Paul said, "And we know that all things work together for good to them that love God, to them who are the called according to his purpose" (Romans 8:28). I pray this book will be a source of encouragement and strength to you as the storms of adversity come your way. I pray you'll find the faith and power to *bend and not break*.

LARRY JONES

10

HOW TO BEND WITHOUT BREAKING

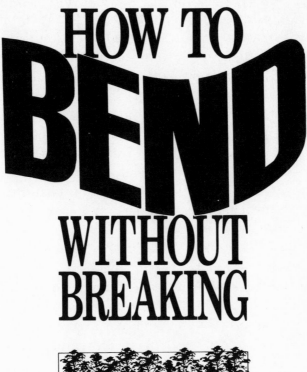

PART

Comeback From Catastrophe:

Healing the damage caused by sudden storms

Failure:

How to turn it to your advantage

Failure doesn't mean God wasn't there; it means He may have a better purpose for you.

When Evelyn told me about her plans, she talked so fast I could hardly understand her. I hadn't seen her so excited in a long time. After a lifetime of trying to please her mother and always failing, she had finally found something she just knew would make her mother happy. For years, her mother had fantasized about visiting her old home community in Arkansas and reliving a very special time she had experienced years ago with her favorite son, who was now deceased.

With a courage she had not felt in years, Evelyn made all the travel plans and then announced the surprise to her mother. The next day, they left for Arkansas, full of anticipation and excitement.

But the festive mood was short-lived. Before they were even out of her home town, Evelyn got lost, taking a freeway route that took them several miles out of the way. By the time they were back on the right road, they were both tense and irritable.

It was dark when they finally arrived in the small

Arkansas community and, much to Evelyn's dismay, the motel room she had reserved had already been given to someone else. Fighting back the tears, Evelyn drove to another motel, which was not up to her standards, but available just the same.

The next morning, they drove out to see the old farm place only to discover that a lake completely covered the site and the small farming community no longer existed. Their planned reunion with a very meaningful past could not be. There was nothing to do but turn back and head for home.

The return drive was long, the air filled with disappointment and disapproval. More than once, Evelyn's mother complained about being taken on a "wild goose chase," and how tired she was.

Evelyn was devastated. Again, she had failed to gain her mother's approval. "I'll never try again," she said through her tears. "I'm a failure and I'll always be a failure."

John Greenleaf Whittier once wrote, "Of all sad words of tongue or pen, the saddest are these: 'It might have been.' " That's the essence of failure, isn't it? . . . having something within our grasp and then losing it . . . knowing that success was just a mistake or two away. These were Evelyn's feelings.

By whose standards are you judging yourself? Anytime you discuss failure, you have to decide by what standards the failure is judged. Certainly, as a tour guide Evelyn was a failure. She couldn't even get out of town! Yet, as a daughter trying to express love to her mother, she definitely wasn't a failure.

Even Jesus' days on earth could be judged as unsuccessful by some standards. He was a failure in the eyes of the Romans. He was a failure in the eyes of religious leaders. He was a failure in the eyes of His peers. By virtually every indicator, He was a giant failure. He was killed almost before He got started. The reason was clear: He walked to a different drumbeat. He was to do His Father's will. He did not let the standards of success of others detour Him from His own path. He accomplished His mission and the effects are still felt today.

Take a look at your own goals. You may be losing at somebody else's game, but succeeding in ways that really matter. I've talked with "successful men" who have failed as husbands and fathers. They have failed at their most important tasks, yet, because they've made a great deal of money, they think they are successful.

Christ expects us to improve and to have room for change. The Apostle John wrote, "But as many as received him, to them gave he power to become the sons of God, even to them that believe on his name" (John 1:12). We're promised the power to "become." That means we haven't yet accomplished all we can be or hope to be, but Christ won't give up on us. And we shouldn't give up on ourselves.

1. Failure doesn't mean you've lost.

History is replete with stories of great people who saw themselves as failures. Impressionist painter Vincent van Gogh died without ever knowing that his bold and colorful paintings were masterful works of art. Afflicted with chronic depression, van Gogh lived out the last days of his life convinced he was a failure. Unable to stand the torment, he borrowed a revolver and shot himself. Even that drastic act was not successful. "I have failed again," he told his brother Theo. Two days later he died.

Today, van Gogh's paintings hang in galleries world-wide. These priceless masterpieces were painted by a man who died thinking of himself as a failure!

The stories of Evelyn and van Gogh are very different. Yet, in a way, they're just the same: The failure was not in the acting, but in their perception of how the act was received. Evelyn and van Gogh both perceived that their actions were failures. The responses they received reinforced that belief. In reality, they did not fail. They simply didn't get the appropriate responses they needed at the time.

That lack of a proper response is one of the reasons most of us give up so easily when we think we have failed. We quit too soon! But, those who succeed never give up until they find something or someone who will give them a positive response to the things they're trying to achieve.

2. Failure doesn't mean you haven't tried; it means you haven't tried everything.

Probably the most famous example of this is the story told about Thomas Edison, who tried hundreds of experiments in his quest for a filament that would work in his light bulb. Time after time, the experiments failed. "Aren't you discouraged?" his assistant asked after a particularly trying day.

"No," said Edison, "I've just learned more things that won't work." He kept trying until he found just the right material that made his invention work.

There is no one in the world who is achieving anything who isn't also running the risk of failure. The successful person is the person who refuses to be defeated by his failures. Every person pays a price either in prestige, dollars, energy, or emotional output.

In the entire history of baseball, there's never been a

hitter who batted 1.000 every day at bat. There's never been a pitcher who has struck out every batter he faced during his whole career. Everybody fails at one time or another. The point is that we can't let our failures defeat us. We must be willing to pay the price to succeed.

3. Failure doesn't mean it's time to give up; it means success will come another time.

The great Turkish conqueror, Tamerlane, was once forced to hide from his enemies in a ruined building where he sat alone for many hours.

He later recalled, "Desiring to divert my mind from my hopeless condition, I fixed my eyes on an ant that was carrying a grain of corn larger than itself up a high wall. I numbered the efforts it made to accomplish this object. The grain fell sixty-nine times to the ground; but the insect persevered, and the seventieth time it reached the top. This sight gave me courage at the moment, and I never forgot the lesson."

We need rest stops along the road of life, intermissions before the next main event. If you were traveling from Chicago to Los Angeles and after the first day you still had a thousand miles to go, you wouldn't consider your travel a failure. Rather, you'd realize you had another couple of day's travel to go.

Life is much the same. Our goals cannot all be accomplished in one fell swoop. There are milestones along the way and rest stops that we need to make. Today's pause may be tomorrow's needed refreshment.

4. Failure doesn't mean you should be embarrassed; it means you had the courage to try.

Carl Sandburg has told the story about Abe Lincoln at the age of seven. One evening Abe walked over to his cabin door and opened it. He looked up onto the face of the full moon and said, "Mr. Moon, what do you see from way up there?"

Mr. Moon answered, "Abe, I see a calendar and it says 1816. I see eight million people in the United States of America. I see 16,000 covered wagons plodding slowly across the midwestern plains toward California. And, Abe, I see far to the west a wagon in the desert between two ridges of the Rocky Mountains. The wagon is broken, weeds are crawling in the spokes, and there is an old dusty skeleton nearby with a pair of moccasins and some dry bones. I also see a sign that says, 'The cowards never started!' "

The very fact that you're experiencing failure is a compliment to you—you had the courage to stick your neck out and try something. With this attitude, you can face the failures that will inevitably come, and you'll also keep trying until you succeed.

5. Failure doesn't mean God wasn't there; it means He may have had a better purpose for you.

In the sixteenth chapter of Acts is the marvelous story of the Apostle Paul's inability to get God's approval of the places he wanted to evangelize. Paul first wanted to go to Asia, but he was "forbidden of the Holy Ghost to preach the word in Asia" (verse 6). Next, after entering into Mysia, "they assayed to go into Bithynia: but the Spirit suffered them not" (verse 7). Finally, after they were in Troas, Paul had a vision in the night in which "there stood a man of Macedonia, and prayed him, saying, Come over into Macedonia, and help us" (verse 9).

This was not Paul's first choice. But God had another purpose and plan for him: Paul's second choice. Paul had failed to find the doors opened to Asia and Bithynia, because God had a better purpose for him. Because Paul was willing to follow God's plan, the Gospel eventually came to Europe and many centuries later to America. What looked like failure at the moment was better than if Paul had succeeded with his own plans.

As He was being crucified, Jesus cried out to His Father, the words of failure on His lips. His chosen disciples had abandoned Him; His teachings had been ridiculed; He was dying a horrible death. And in His moment of rejection on the cross, He cried out, "My God, my God, why hast thou forsaken me?" (Matthew 27:46.)

I'm sure you've had desperate feelings of rejection in your own moments of failure. Maybe you have felt that even God has forsaken you. But as surely as Jesus was resurrected from the dead, you can find a new life even in the midst of failures. "In everything you do, put God first, and he will direct you and crown your efforts with success" (Proverbs 3:6 TLB).

I once planned a march across Oklahoma and Kansas to collect grain for our feeding programs and to call attention to the massive amount of surplus grain we have stored in our country's elevators. I expected large crowds at our nightly meetings, because we were traveling through areas where many of our best supporters lived.

On the third night, I decided that I had really made a mistake. Crowds were small; news coverage was sparse, and I began to feel we had failed. I was so discouraged I almost cancelled the remainder of the march. But something told me not to quit too soon. As I started listening to the few people who came out to the meetings, I began to realize that our friends and farm supporters weren't coming out to see us because they didn't want us to see them in bad financial straits. Many had given us grain through the years, but now they couldn't even afford a small offering for the ministry. So, we changed horses in midstream! I stopped taking offerings and became concerned about helping the farmers we met on the march. I stopped talking about my needs and started listening to theirs. Proverbs 21:13 states, "Whoso stoppeth his ears at the cry of the poor, he also shall cry himself, but shall not be heard." When I started listening to the cries of the farmers and got involved in their problems, the whole march turned around.

By the end of the eight-day event, God had used us to call attention to problems that were more important than the ones we had started with, and the march was a great success. We produced a national television special about the farm problem that rallied thousands of supporters for the farmers' problems. All that happened because we didn't quit too soon.

6. Temporary failure may lead to permanent success.

I'll never forget visiting with an elderly gentleman who had endured more than fifty surgical procedures. Yet, he had one of the most healthy emotional attitudes I had ever seen.

"How do you keep such a positive attitude when you've suffered so much?" I asked.

His answer was worth remembering: "The surgeries are just temporary inconveniences. Inside, I'm still me."

That's an important lesson to learn. No matter what happens, nothing can take away your value as a human being. The sport of baseball does something each year which underscores this lesson. Each year, the "Comeback Player of the Year" award is given to some athlete who had been down on his luck, who had not been performing well, but who now had made a significant turnaround. You may feel you're "washed up"—maybe some people have written you off as a failure—but inside you're still the same person who has often succeeded at many things you tried. No one can take that away. You may be in for your own "Comeback of the Year" award.

God wants to teach you this lesson. You're not a failure; in fact, you've not ever really failed. You've simply had a lot of learning opportunities. God is for you. "If God be for us, who can be against us?" (Romans 8:31). Believe it; receive it—now.

LESSONS FROM THE TREES

The American chestnut blight

The American chestnut was once one of the most important eastern hardwood trees. It was highly prized for its delicious chestnuts and its beautifully grained wood, which was versatile and durable. Chestnut blight, a fungus that destroys the living tissue beneath the bark, has virtually wiped out the American chestnut tree. The disease was first discovered in New York in 1904, probably entering this country on an imported Asiatic chestnut nursery tree. Within fifty years, the blight had spread throughout the entire natural range of the American chestnut, killing more than nine million acres of chestnut forests.

Fortunately, the chestnut tree has fought off extinction because new sprouts continue to grow from the roots of long-dead trees. These sprouts often become large enough to produce chestnuts before the blight kills them. Botanists are hopeful that eventually the American chestnut will make a comeback. They are currently experimenting with hybrids between the American chestnut and blight-resistant Chinese chestnuts. Perhaps even a strain of naturally blight-resistant American chestnuts may someday be found.

Sometimes, failure can result in feelings as devastating and fatal as chestnut blight. Unchecked, a sense of failure can destroy everything in its path—the joy, the courage, the essence of living a fulfilled life.

If failures, real or merely perceived, are threatening to destroy you, take a lesson from the chestnut tree. Learn to see your failures as temporary setbacks, not permanent failures. Don't lose heart. And don't allow bitterness to leave a path of hollowness and destruction in your life. *Bend, don't break.* Take the steps to change, remove bitterness before it wreaks its awful toll, and, like the chestnut, you'll be on your way to eventual victory over your failures.

2

How to regain your
self-esteem

"I didn't have a choice in whether I was fired, but I do have a choice as to how I react to that firing. I had a lot of good years here, and I do have a lot of good years left. I will land on my own two feet."

FRED AKERS
Former football coach,
University of Texas

I still remember the front page of a metropolitan newspaper which pictured a family of four sleeping on one mattress on the floor of a mission house. The father had lost his job in a small farm town and had come to the city in hopes of finding employment.

Feed the Children went out to the mission to see if we could help them. What we found broke my heart. Sitting on a bed that all four shared, the father and mother talked about how hard it was to work their way out of the situation they were in. With no money, the father couldn't buy gas for his car and without transportation, he couldn't search for a job. Even when he did apply, he found most places were looking for people with skills he did not have. The mother, still concerned about the health and cleanliness of her two young daughters, was worried that the girls were not getting the right food. Besides, a mission was no place for two little girls to live. They had no place to play, and no room to move around in but a four-foot by four-foot space.

Can you imagine what it's like not knowing where your next meal is coming from? Or if there's even going to be a next meal? Even worse, not being able to provide for your spouse and children?

In our American social and economic system, hardly anything is more emotionally jarring than the loss of a job. A job means income. Loss of income means inability to buy. Eventually, this results in loss of credit and loss of savings. Added to these very practical considerations is the loss of identity and self-esteem. It's almost impossible not to question one's self-worth when something as important as a job is suddenly taken away. I have seen presidents of large companies, competent and confident people, who have gradually become immobilized after they were removed from their positions of power.

Although it's tough for everyone, it is probably hardest emotionally for men. That's not to say that the effects aren't the same for everyone and just as difficult, but in America, men are programmed from childhood to be something—to be a fireman, a policeman, a minister, a farmer, an athlete, or a doctor. Boys are taught that their worth and identity are wrapped up in their work. Unemployment not only reduces a man's income, it also attacks his identity and self-worth.

Though the vocation of women has been emphasized for more than two decades, the connection between self-identity and a job is still way out of proportion for men. But whether man or woman, when the work is needed and it is no longer there, the results can be devastating.

The American economy has been so strong over the past fifty years that most of us haven't experienced the trauma of not being able to feed our families. We read the stories of starvation and hunger overseas and don't often think about such things happening to us. Nevertheless, each day the list of personal bankruptcies increases, the mission houses get fuller, banks fail, and businesses close down.

Many people break under the pressure of losing their source of income. The collapse of the stock market in the Great Depression of 1929 is proof of that. We all have heard stories of people jumping out of windows or committing suicide in other dramatic ways when they discovered they were suddenly broke. In 1986, in Edmond, Oklahoma, a troubled postal employee, fearing loss of his job, walked into the post office one morning and shot fourteen of his fellow employees, before turning the gun on himself. This senseless massacre was perpetrated by a man who broke under the threat of unemployment.

I've watched people loosen a barrage of anger and rage that they later regretted. In their loss of control, they burned bridges that could have been helpful later on in their search for a new job. That is why it is important for anyone experiencing a traumatic job change to self-impose a cooling-down period. This allows time for anger, frustration, guilt, and other negative emotions to dissipate. The prophet Isaiah said it another way: "In returning and rest shall ye be saved; in quietness and in confidence shall be your strength . . ." (Isaiah 30:15).

The biblical character Joseph is an excellent illustration of how time can smooth out the rough paths of turmoil and injustice. Joseph was sold into slavery by his own brothers. A woman he had befriended lied about his character and integrity and he was imprisoned. Yet, in the midst of his suffering at the hands of someone else's wrongdoing, he maintained a quiet strength that later allowed him to rise above his past and move into an even brighter future as ruler of all those who had wronged him. When his brothers who had sold him into slavery stood before him, Joseph was able to say, "You meant evil for me; God meant good." (*See* Genesis 50:20.) That's another way of saying, "When a window closes, God opens a door." When one job goes, we need to keep on looking for another, discovering the new thing God has in store for us.

It's important to look at unemployment as a temporary pause, not as a stop sign. We cannot allow ourselves the luxury of beginning to think of ourselves as a "fired" or "unemployed" person. Once we do that, an insidious disease spreads through our body and causes us to think of ourselves as less than capable, less than we really are. Even though we may be without a job, as long as we face each day with the confidence and assurance that comes from faith in God and faith in the talents He's given us, we can make it.

Here are some suggestions that have been given to persons without work:

1. Never think of yourself as being identified by the job you've had.

You may be a fireman or president of a company by profession, but that is not who you are. You are a human being created by God and loved by Him. You have marvelous capacities and capabilities. None of these are diminished by any external circumstance. Your potential to grow and change is not limited by the way other people evaluate or judge you. You are the only one who can curb your potential, and you do that by narrowing the scope by which you see yourself. When one door closes, it marks the end of that opportunity. But the number of doors that may eventually open up to you, if you're willing to consider all doors, is unlimited. As we grow older it becomes harder to make critical life changes. It may become necessary—and even a challenging opportunity—to think of all the new job and career possibilities that are now available.

I recently talked with a farmer who had lost his farm and his profession along with it. His daughter enrolled in college that same year, and it occurred to the unemployed farmer that he could do the same thing, so he did! If he couldn't be a farmer any longer, he could learn to do something new. And so can you!

2. Accept that there are simply some things we can't control.

A farmer cannot control what's happening in the economy. He can be active and responsible; he can make his voice heard; but ultimately, there's little he can do about world markets and their effect on his small farm in middle America.

A steelworker can't stop the flow of foreign imports or modernize an old plant. Oil people are dependent on decisions made in Saudi Arabia and other dominant oil-producing countries that dramatically affect the price of oil. Manufacturers of soft goods have little if any control over labor costs in Third World countries. In spite of everything they do to cut their own costs, shoe manufacturers, for example, simply cannot compete with companies who produce shoes with cheap labor and can therefore sell them at reduced costs.

Accepting the limitations of what you can and cannot control will keep you from expending energy trying to change situations that are beyond your power to change. It will also encourage you to spend your time in positive and successful ways.

3. Remember that although you don't have control over what happens in the workplace, you do have control over how you respond to it.

There will be nothing more destructive to you than responding to a job loss by lashing back. You can blame your employer or the economy or the government from now until doomsday, and it won't change a thing. Lashing out is destructive to you because there is a boomerang effect to negative criticism. It's like a mirror that reflects our image back at us. All that negative energy hits the mirror and comes back on us so that we feel like we've been drenched by it.

It's difficult to maintain emotional control when you think someone may have intentionally hurt you, but the ability to discipline your feelings will allow you to *bend and not break* when you face this crisis. You can't determine what people do to you, but you can control how you react to them.

A friend of mine used to be head of a state corrections work program. Although he had little training in the field of corrections, he got the job after working with the agency in a consulting capacity. They were impressed with his managerial skills and asked him to serve as interim director for one year. But, before he could assume the position, the man who had created the work release program was demoted and in effect released of every responsibility that mattered.

"I was terribly uncomfortable the first time I met this man in the hall," said my friend. "In his mind, he had done a superior job for the state, and now they had rewarded him by putting someone like me, a novice, in his place."

But, the next morning, this man did something that surprised my friend. A cup of coffee in his hand, his pride under control, he walked into my friend's office, the office he used to occupy, and sat down.

"I want to help you," he said sincerely. "You didn't have anything to do with my demotion. If they hadn't hired you, they would have hired someone else."

During my friend's one-year stay, no one was more helpful than this man—a man who couldn't control what had happened to him, but could decide how to react.

Alexander Graham Bell said, "When one door closes, another opens. But we often look so long and so regretfully upon the closed door, that we do not see the one that is open."

4. Concentrate on letting God support you spiritually during this time.

Ask for God's strength and support as you struggle with the realities facing you. Ask Him for courage to go through the difficult task of finding something else to do. Ask Him for help with your depression and your loss of identity. He knows and He cares; trust Him.

The Apostle Paul learned to seek solace in his faith when times got tough. And who had more setbacks than this servant of God? "Though our outward man perish, yet the inward man is renewed day by day," he wrote in 2 Corinthians 4:16.

Though it may be difficult for you now, know that God is present to support you during your hour of trial. When it seems that you've withstood all the pressures and failures you can stand, lean on Him, accept the quiet renewal of inner strength that His love can give you. You have the opportunity to live your faith to the fullest, to *bend without breaking!*

LESSONS FROM THE TREES

Oak wilt

Oak wilt is a tree disease related to Dutch elm disease. It enters the oak tree through wounds and then spreads rapidly throughout the entire tree. Left untreated, a powerful oak can be totally destroyed. Very few varieties of oak can survive the onslaught of oak wilt.

In the same way, I've seen strong men and women devastated over the loss of their jobs. And until it has happened to you, it's hard to realize its far-reaching implications—bills, mortgage payments, medical insurance, savings, kids, food, the future, all become grim priorities when the job is gone. The regular check is no longer there.

Wounded and weak, we become vulnerable to attack from without. Left unattended, a wound can become infected and festered. That's why we have to treat it promptly and thereby protect ourselves from the potential ravages of disease. Unfortunately, many turn to drugs and alcohol when they face unemployment. Others become abusive and bitter. They break instead of bend. But if we face the wound that's been made and acknowledge the need not to be bitter, we can keep the loss from breaking us. We can keep strong spiritually, and with God's help we can face whatever the future may hold. If Christ helped you take the last step, then He will help you take the next one.

3

Financial Disaster:

Finding the silver lining behind a very dark cloud

"You can do what you can for as long as you can, and when you finally can't, you do the next best thing. You back up, but you don't give up."

CHUCK YEAGER

I visited sometime back with a sixty-year-old farmer and businessman. He said, "Larry, I've farmed all of my life. Now I've lost my farm, and I'm sixty years old. My boy was my partner and he's thirty-seven. He may be able to find another trade. But who wants an out-of-work sixty-year-old farmer?"

He wasn't alone. Since 1982, more than 300,000 farm families have lost their farms. And the emotional strain they face is often unbearable. In December, 1985, Iowa farmer Dale Burr broke under the strain of losing his farm and livelihood. In utter desperation, he killed his banker, a neighboring farmer, his wife, and finally himself. And there are many others like Dale Burr who break under the severity of the crises they face. In my home state of Oklahoma, tragic reports of farm-related suicides by farmers and even their wives continue to call our attention to the problem. Crisis hotlines for farm families are being flooded with calls from farmers who are emotionally depressed and in need of support. The irony is that farm families, who for years have produced food for the nation and the world, are so financially strapped that they are being forced to ask for welfare and food stamps.

Many become so bitter they spend all their energies fighting events which happened in the past, events over which they have no control nor power to change. For some, that attitude is pushing them to the breaking point. But it is possible to *bend and not break*, even in the face of an overwhelming set of circumstances.

One of the best examples I know is the Wyler family in Tonkowa, Oklahoma. I had met the Wylers during a 228-mile march from Wichita, Kansas, to Oklahoma City—a march intended to make the public aware of the vast surpluses of grain we have stored in our nation's elevators. As we passed through Tonkowa, the Wylers had just been told that their farm would be sold at auction. They invited me to come back and be with them at the sale.

I arrived early the day of the auction. It was not a happy time. If it hadn't been for the farm auction sign out front, you would have thought people were gathering for a funeral wake. Those coming walked slowly, almost respectfully, talking in hushed tones as they arrived in their pickup trucks and vans. A few huddled together in small groups, quietly discussing what was about to take place. Others stood alone, their feet shifting uncomfortably, almost embarrassed at even being there.

Quentin Wyler's brother and sisters had been reared on

the home place. "We had a lot of good times here," his brother said, fighting to hold back the tears. Even the school they had all attended was located on the farm—it was the same school their father and grandfather had attended before them.

"It's just like losing a member of the family," said Quentin's mother, Wanna Wyler. "This farm's been in our family for eighty years, and now we're losing it. I just wish it weren't happening."

But, it did. To the singsong sounds of the auctioneer, one by one, the trucks and farm equipment and eventually the house and land were sold. By mid-afternoon, the auction was over. Many drove away apprehensively, wondering if they, too, would soon suffer the same fate that Quentin and Kathy Wyler had just endured.

When everyone had left, I went into the kitchen where the family had gathered. It was a place where they had all shared some good times. But no more. We talked and I did my best to minister to them. Then when it was time to leave, we joined hands to pray. I said, "Lord, don't let this family become bitter. Give them the strength to overcome this experience, the courage to begin a new life, and the grace to forgive themselves and others who have been involved in this painful loss."

We all said, "Amen." After a while, I said good-bye. I left believing the Wylers will make it. I believe they'll live through the loss of their home without letting bitterness ruin their future.

As I've talked to people like the Wylers, to farmers, bankers, oilmen, steelworkers, and people in all sectors of our economy who are reeling under the impact of our nation's problems, it seems to me there are several things that are important to remember:

1. Life isn't fair, but we have divine recourse.

If you think life should be fair, you'll be butting your head against the wall the rest of your days.

- It's not fair that our country provides millions of dollars in aid directly and indirectly to Argentina. Then that country uses the money to subsidize its farmers' wheat crops, allowing them to undercut American wheat sixty cents a bushel in world markets.

- It's not fair what has happened to the oil industry. When the Arabs raised their price per barrel, Americans by the thousands began a massive effort to find new oil sources for our nation. People invested their money in drilling rigs, sold leases, and tried new and innovative techniques for increasing our oil supply, thereby decreasing our dependence on foreign oil. Hardly had this happened when the bottom of the market dropped out. In states like Texas, Oklahoma, and Louisiana, the oil industry was dealt a crippling blow. Thousands of people who had committed themselves to solving the oil crisis were hit equally hard. Now all across the "oil patch," rigs lie rusting, marginal wells are being capped, and thousands of workers have been laid off. Businesses, banks, and savings and loan organizations are also suffering as a result of the downturn in energy.

- It's not fair that President Carter stopped the sale of wheat to Russia over the invasion of Afghanistan. That decision caused Russia to turn to other marketplaces. It destroyed the American wheat market and it didn't hurt the Russians one whit! There were a lot of other options, but Carter's uninformed choice made only the farmers pay the penalty.

- It's not fair that Congress has been unwilling to cut spending which allowed inflation to race away. The result was soaring land prices. When farmers borrowed against their land, they used those inflated prices as collateral. When inflation was halted, land prices fell and the value of the farmers' collateral disappeared.

- And the list goes on—fuel, fertilizer, implements, and interest rates. For these the farmer has paid the price.

Probably more than any group in our country today, farmers have been forced to recognize that long hours of honest, hard work may not pay off in the end.

One farmer told me that for years he had subsidized his wheat operation with the sale of calves from his herd of cattle. Even when the wheat crop failed, he could always count on the calves to pull him through another year. This year, however, right when it was time to sell his heifers, the government allowed dairy farmers to flood the market with their dairy cows, and the bottom dropped out of the cattle market. A year's worth of time, money, and work were wasted. None of it was his fault, yet he suffered the consequences. This was the same man who went around to all his neighbors and collected more than $2,000 to help us buy grain for starving children overseas. Close to bankruptcy on the outside, he would not allow his spirit to become "bankrupt" on the inside even though life had treated him unfairly.

A few miles away, another young farmer who had

suffered much the same experience, said, "I've learned to rethink what's really important to me. Family, friends, and a real relationship with God—those are most important."

It's most important to know that God is on your side. One of the great stories of the Old Testament, loved by children and adults alike, is the account of the battle between David and Goliath. If ever there was an unfair match, that was. Goliath had everything on his side; David seemingly had nothing. David was not as concerned about what Goliath threatened to do to him as he was about experiencing what God was going to do for him. David turned to God for help, and in so doing, he maximized the divine and minimized the human. He put God on his side and thereby had more on his side than Goliath could ever hope to have on his. For "if God be for us, who can be against us?" We know the results of the battle: David and God won.

I've always liked the statement, "Without God, I cannot; without me, He will not." In the midst of your struggle, God may be your most important resource. In fact, bringing God into the picture may be the only way you will resolve the financial dilemmas you're confronting. If you're facing Goliath, remember what David did: he weighted the odds in his favor by turning to God for help. If it worked for him, it will work for you.

Equally as important when the bottom falls out, remember this:

2. Back up, but don't give up.

Chuck Yeager is one of America's premier test pilots and the man who flew an airplane faster than the speed of sound for the first time. For that courageous feat, achieved when he was twenty-four years old, Yeager was awarded a Special Congressional Silver Medal.

Yeager knew that the flight doctor would never let him in the plane if he told the medic that he had broken two ribs two days before the monumental test in the X-1, so he said nothing and took off in great pain. He went on to new achievements and his work has blazed the trail for America's space program.

Today, well into his sixties, he still flies high-performance aircraft. In his autobiography, Yeager has this to say: "If the day comes when a flight surgeon tells me I can't fly anymore in high-performance jets, I can always sneak out back and fly ultra-lights. You do what you can for as long as you can, and when you finally can't you do the next best thing. You back up, but you don't give up."

It may mean we have to redirect our lives and accept that some changes have occurred over which we have no control. But God didn't bring you this far to let you fail. He is with you all the way.

3. What looks like the end of the road may be a turn in the road.

I remember my own painful experience when we lost seventy-five percent of our employees as a result of a situation totally out of my control. My ministry had just begun to flourish, when without warning three-fourths of the people I'd trained and worked with left. I had a lot of "whys." I lay awake at night wondering what I could have done which would have prevented the problem from occurring. I felt like a failure. But, I learned from this and other experiences to deal with the feelings of failure.

As actress Mary Pickford said, "What looks like the end

of the road in our personal experience is only the turn in the road, the beginning of a new and more beautiful journey." Yet, anytime you work hard to succeed—and it fails in spite of everything you do—it's hard to overcome the sense of bitterness that creeps in and reminds you that you've worked so hard for nothing.

In the southwestern part of the United States, a tremendous number of businesses have failed during the past five years due to the decline in the oil industry. Banks have closed; farms have been auctioned off; the spiral of a falling economy is affecting countless other businesses and industries. I've stood by helplessly as friends, who at one time were wealthy people, have been forced to give up their homes and cards, and worst of all, their pride and self-esteem.

Many have become bitter because they think they're too old to start over or they don't know where to begin again. Their successes have been measured in dollars and cents, and they don't know how to think of themselves without that crutch of money. They hide—some with drugs and alcohol, some with new wives and life-styles. Yet, sooner or later, they'll have to begin the difficult task of rebuilding their lives, letting go of the bitterness of failure, and looking at ways to begin again.

I have a friend in eastern Oklahoma who for years had been a successful contractor and developer. When hard times came to Oklahoma, his contracting business went to pieces. When I was visiting with him recently, I learned, to my surprise, that he was in the coal-mining business. I asked him, "How in the world did you get into coal mining?"

"Well," he said, "I didn't have much choice. When building shut down, I began to look around for something else to do, and I heard someone say something about coal mining. I checked into it a little, found some land, and began mining it. It's as simple as that. Instead of seeing my business going under as a stop sign, I just made it into a detour, and went from contracting to coal mining."

During the Depression of the 1930s, J. C. Penney was struggling to keep his stores open, and it looked as if he would fail. In the midst of this personal financial crisis, he became very sick and went into the hospital. One night, plummeting in despair, he became so convinced that his life was over that he wrote a letter to his wife and children, not expecting to be alive the next morning. But, when the early morning rays of the sun shone into his room, Mr. Penney was awakened by the strains of an old hymn that was running though his mind:

> *Be not dismayed whate'er betide,*
> *God will take care of you;*
> *Beneath His wings of love abide,*
> *God will take care of you.*
> *No matter what may be the test,*
> *God will take care of you;*
> *Lean, weary one, upon His breast,*
> *God will take care of you.*

As the comforting words of that song filled his room, J. C. Penney sat up in bed, determined to defeat the failures that were tormenting him. His simple, yet strong faith in God would sustain him throughout his long life. What looked like a dead end was really only a turn in the road. That may well be what God is trying to tell you now. Look at the road that seems to have ended as only a turn that you need to make.

4. When you hit bottom, there's only one option left—up.

During Civil War days, there was a man in Louisiana named Edmund McIlhenny who owned a sugar plantation and saltworks. Like most able-bodied men, he had to leave home and go to war. When he returned, there was nothing but a pile of ruins to welcome him back. As he stood surveying his loss, he felt totally abandoned, with no future, no options, and no possibilities.

After awhile, he noticed something growing at his feet. It was a few Mexican peppers that had somehow reseeded themselves in what had at one time been a flourishing garden. Not having anything else to do, he started experimenting with those peppers. He picked some of them and made a sauce out of them. It tasted so good that he decided to make some more. He washed out some discarded cologne bottles he found in the rubble and put his sauce inside them.

Eventually, he sold some of his sauce to a few friends. They kept coming back for more, and soon he had a little business going. Today McIlhenny's "Tabasco Sauce" is on the shelves of grocery stores across America. It's still in a container that looks like those old cologne bottles from long ago. From the ashes of a sugar plantation came a Tabasco company.

What are the options for you now that one door has been closed? Failing at a business may have filled you with bitterness, but you don't have to be defeated. As surely as oil prices fall, as surely as famine moves across a land unexpectedly, as surely as "sure things" fail—just as certainly you can be sure that God will be your rock, your fortress, your deliverer. "My God, my strength, in whom I will trust; my buckler, and the horn of my salvation, and my high tower" (Psalm 18:2).

God has a new opportunity for every one of us. It may not be what we dreamed of, or what we wanted most, or what seems would have been best. But it is our opportunity and one we must find in the ashes of our defeat. "Our greatest glory is not in never falling," said British author Oliver Goldsmith, "but in rising every time we fall." One thing's sure: when we have hit bottom, there's only one way to go—up. That's the way God wants you to go. Remember, a tree bends over during the storm, but after the storm it straightens up.

5. When disaster hits, start over as quickly as possible.

When an earthquake hit Mexico City in 1985, I went there to see in what way Feed the Children could be of assistance. The quake had left a nightmare of gigantic proportions. Buildings were reduced to rubble. Businesses had vanished. And worst of all were the countless thousands in shock and disbelief searching desperately for their loved ones.

The thing that impressed me most about the Mexican people and their government was the way they approached this disaster: they were not sitting around in despair; rather, they were working as fast as possible to clear the rubble, to rebuild, to find new ways to build a new life. They weren't denying the tragedy, but were doing the very opposite: accepting it and committing to starting over.

That is the best advice for you in your situation: *start over.* Don't deny the past; learn any lesson it has to offer. Take immediate steps to begin again; and when you do, I'm confident that new answers and new directions will begin to multiply.

In Proverbs 3:5, 6, these words give great encouragement: "Trust in the Lord with all thine heart; and lean not unto thine own understanding. In all thy ways acknowledge him, and he shall direct thy paths."

LESSONS FROM THE TREES

Transplanting

Transplanting a tree successfully requires more than simply moving it from one place to another. It must be moved in such a way that allows the tree to continue to grow. That means minimizing the amount of shock to the tree from being uprooted, as well as insuring its future ability to grow and develop with the least possible interruption. To do that means giving careful attention to three areas of concern: how the tree is uprooted (roots are always kept moist and protected during the transplanting); how the new location site is prepared (appropriate preparation of the new soil will minimize the shock); and finally, how the tree is replanted (maximum care and concern are always called for).

Like trees, our lives at times have to be uprooted. Financial disaster can hit, leaving us little of the security we previously knew. When that happens, the trees can teach us an important lesson: Life is not over because our lives have been uprooted. There is life after financial disaster. But as in the transplanting of trees, there are three things we should be concerned with: how we left our old situation (did we burn our bridges or leave the doors open for future communication?); how our new spot is prepared (it's new and different, but it's our new place, so it needs to be treated carefully); and our commitment to grow even when we've been forced to "transplant" our lives into a new situation. Life can even be better than it ever was before!

4

Divorce:

Living with a new reality

"I'll stand in the gap with you until you either reclaim your family or until you're strong enough to stand alone."

A friend of a divorcée

I t was a classic case. Jim and Pam met and married in college. She worked while he completed medical school. For twenty-one years, they shared children and dreams. And, then, in classic mid-life crisis style, the successful doctor turned to another woman, and Pam found herself in the middle of a nightmare unlike any crisis she had ever experienced.

A woman of considerable faith, Pam turned to the church and to a few close friends who came forward to offer comfort and support. But one friend did more than lend a shoulder to cry on; she presented Pam with a challenge. "If you're strong enough," she said, "you may be able to withstand this attack on your family and bridge the gap that has torn your family apart." Then, she promised, "I'll stand in the gap with you until you either reclaim your family or until you're strong enough to stand alone."

It wasn't easy for Pam. She hated being "neither fish nor fowl." She was married but her husband was living with another woman. Days, weeks, and months passed. Her friends stood in the gap with her. They prayed for her, they cried with her, they listened to her. And each time she saw her husband, her only response to their relationship was, "I'm praying for you and for our family."

The last time I heard from Pam, she and her husband were not back together, but there had been progress. He had tired of the younger woman he had been so enamored with. On his own he had gone to a counselor for help. After a while, through the counselor's intercession, he and Pam began meeting to discuss what had happened to their marriage and what future they have.

So far, they're still married, Pam's still praying, and her friends are still standing in the gap with her. As Pam said, "Divorce is the easy way out. I'm determined with God's help to do everything I can to keep this marriage together."

Divorce would not destroy one out of every two marriages in the United States if more couples were willing to "stand in the gap" until their problems could be solved. Vows of "until death us do part" are set aside like old furniture. Divorce has become so common that people even celebrate when their divorces are final. It's viewed as an act of courage and achievement.

One of the most radical changes that has taken place in our country during the last twenty-five years is society's attitude toward divorce. For many years, easy divorce was for celebrities and movie stars who spent the required six weeks in Nevada in order to obtain a divorce. For everyone else, divorce was frowned on in the courts, church, and society at large. Those divorces that were sought could well be long, drawn-out affairs.

Divorce carried an unwanted stigma. Children from broken homes were looked on with pity. There were no "singles' classes" at church. Books extolling the benefits of the single life were not to be found. Divorce was simply not an option.

Unfortunately, like falling dominoes, those attitudes have changed. And, if anything, divorce is too accepted, too easy. Yet, the ease with which a marriage can be dissolved does not carry over into the aftermath of divorce. Only the most calloused and uncaring, those not ever really committed to their families, are able to walk away unscathed, either emotionally or spiritually.

I can't write about divorce without first pleading for anyone who contemplates divorce to consider every option prior to taking that final step. I'm intrigued with the concept of "standing in the gap" that Pam is trying to follow. Rather simply described, she's committed to doing everything within her power to save the marriage, even though her husband is not participating with her. She's listening to his criticisms and acknowledging those faults she can change. She's relating to him with honesty and openness, not judging, not seeking to control. She's trying to understand his disappointments with their life together and to recognize her own.

Without doubt, divorce is one of the major causes of bitterness in America today. Wives and husbands become bitter when the ones they love betray their trust and violate their vows. Children become bitter when the two most important people in their lives behave like lifelong adversaries, feuding and fighting over possessions, money, and even the children they both love. As the poet Langston Hughes so poignantly writes, "When the dreams go, life is a barren field, frozen with snow."

Why do marriages have to break up that way? Why do loved ones break marriage vows and long bonds of trust? Why do people who once loved and cared for each other, sacrificed together, raised children together, even gone to church together, end up in such bitterness?

No matter how young or old you are, being rejected by someone you love is a bitter experience. But, it doesn't have to destroy your life or the lives of those around you. If you face the pain of divorce, these insights will help you:

1. Accept the fact that things will never be the same.

For thousands of families each year, a divorce decree officially signals the breakup of a home. The loss can be a bitter and devastating experience. "It's not that one can never again be happy following an experience of loss," Ann Stearns writes in *Living Through Personal Crisis*. "The reality is simply that one can never again be the same."

Accepting the fact that your life has changed is fundamental to survival. The gap left when any member of the family goes away cannot be closed in an instant. But it does not have to remain an empty void. Through your own power and with the grace of God, you can *bend and not break*.

There once was a man who had purchased a Rolls Royce. A friend of his asked him how much horsepower the engine had. The man didn't know, so he wrote the Rolls Royce company and asked them. Their response was one word: *adequate*. That's also true for the grace of God. It's always adequate.

The psalmist writes, "If I ride the morning winds to the farthest oceans, even there your hand will guide me" (Psalm 139:9, 10 TLB). God's love can sustain you until you're strong enough to stand alone. Accept that promise.

2. Forgive the offending parties.

Forgive? What a difficult thing to do when the wounds of divorce are so fresh and open! How can you forgive someone who has hurt you, someone who has rejected you?

First, begin by forgiving yourself. Rabbi Harold Kushner, in his popular book, *When All You've Ever Wanted Isn't Enough*, says, "One of the worst things that happens to a person who has been hurt by life is that he tends to compound the damage by hurting himself a second time. Not only is he the victim of rejection, bereavement, injury, or bad luck; he often feels the need to see himself as a bad person who had this coming to him, and because of that drives people away, people who try to come close to him and help him." Punishing yourself won't change your situation. Forgiving yourself will!

Secondly, when you forgive those who have hurt you, forgive them completely. Ninety-five percent forgiveness doesn't work. It's like the frequent analogy made about pregnancy—either you're pregnant or you're not.

Forgiving can be very difficult. After the Civil War, an event was scheduled on the White House lawn that brought the warring sides of the North and South together for the first time since the Confederate defeat.

The bandleader went to President Lincoln and asked him what song he should play, thinking Lincoln would suggest a marching favorite of the North. Knowing that the time to build bridges had arrived, Lincoln answered, "Play 'Dixie.' " It was an act of forgiveness and healing that would long be remembered.

Let go of any bitterness that you feel toward the ones who have hurt you. Even Jesus, in talking with the woman at the well who had five husbands, did not judge her. He simply told her about a living water: "Whoever drinks of the water that I shall give . . . will never thirst . . ." (John 4:14 RSV). You can do no less.

I remember going to visit a woman with her pastor. No matter what was said or done, she kept repeating over and over, "No, he won't. No, he won't." Finally, after praying with her, we left. Later, the pastor told me her story as he had learned it. Years ago, her husband had been unfaithful to her. For the duration of their marriage, she had refused to forgive him and she lived in hatred and bitterness until he died. Later, the woman began to regret her bitterness, but she believed that God would never forgive her for failing to forgive her husband. So, she lay in bed, crying over and over, "No, He won't. No, He won't."

One of the family programs I watched on television recently involved a grandfather who was living with his children. One day there came to the door a man who had dated his wife years before. The grandfather became very upset. His grandson asked him, "Granddad, how can you be mad at someone this long?" He answered, "Because I worked at it."

In the same way that you work at carrying a grudge, you have to work at forgiving. We are not given the responsibility of judging any other person's actions. Only God can do that. A simple act of forgiveness will relieve you of a heavy burden and allow you to grow and develop a new life, free of bitterness and anger. It may not be a step that you want to take, but your healing can come only as you bind up wounds and construct new bridges.

3. Believe that there's something left after everything's gone.

I remember counseling with a woman whose abusive husband had died a few months previously. During most of our session, she complained about not being able to do what she wanted. "Harold wouldn't like it," she said. "He never let me do what I wanted to do." Even though Harold was dead, his widow could not let go of the past and accept her own new reality, even though she was now free to do whatever she wanted and had the means to do it.

For most, that possibility is frightening. We like to hang onto whatever is familiar, even when it makes us unhappy and nonproductive people. The fact is, you'll live in an imaginary world, a world that no longer exists, unless you accept your new status. When you cling to something you cannot have, when you cling to a mirage, that's when bitterness and pain force you to the breaking point.

Following the great Chicago fire, a real estate agent put up a sign on the shack which he had constructed after the fire had wiped out everything he owned. It read: "All gone except wife, children, and energy." He wasn't willing to give up, but claimed the new moment and what he had left.

"God grant me the serenity to accept the things I cannot change, the courage to change the things I can, and the wisdom to know the difference." This prayer is prayed everyday by members of Alcoholics Anonymous, and it's a prayer that may help you, too, claim your new reality.

4. Claim the present moment.

Accept the pain. Accept the hurt. These are normal responses to a personal crisis. But, don't build a permanent spot in your heart for those feelings. John Greenleaf Whittier put it this way:

> No longer forward nor behind I look in hope or fear;
> But grateful, take the good I find, The best of now
> and here.

Too often, we hang onto the past, worry about the future, and disregard the present. That's especially true when bitter experiences from the past dominate our lives and keep us from seeing the potential of the present.

Sometimes divorce can shadow your past and put a cloud over your future. In the midst of our pain, we sit idle like a car that's running but not in gear. What we need to do is to put it in drive and start easing forward. The journey of a thousand miles begins with the first step. The first step is in claiming the present moment by telling yourself: *I will not sit. I will through Christ claim this moment.*

Look around you. What gifts, what strengths are still intact, untarnished by the divorce that has shattered you? Those resources are available to you right at this very moment and they can help you *bend and not break*, if you will claim them as your very own.

5. Give yourself time to heal.

Cicero said, "There is no grief which time does not lessen and soften." Time is a very important healing agent. It allows the scars of loss to heal. Accept the pain and hurt that come from losing a love, but don't allow those bitter feelings to grow. Give time a chance to smooth out the peaks of despair until you can cope with the loss. Give your feelings time to heal before you rush into another relationship. Trying to prove you're desirable to another person will only retard the healing process, and unresolved feelings about your lost love could be a detriment to a new relationship.

The writer of Ecclesiastes spoke wisely when he said, "To every thing there is a season, and a time to every purpose under the heaven . . . A time to weep, and a time to laugh; a time to mourn, and a time to dance" (3:1, 4). Give yourself time to heal.

6. Dare to love again.

Late one night, I received a telephone call from a thirty-eight-year-old divorcée. She was crying so hard I could hardly understand her words. For several months, she had dated a very wealthy man who had treated her like a queen. They dined in romantic places; he bought her gifts; they were in love. For her, it was a match made in heaven. But, without warning, he walked in one evening and said he was going back to his former girl-friend, and he walked out the door forever. Hurt and bitter, she vowed never to trust another man again.

Loving is a risk. If you love another, there is always the chance that person will leave you. If you trust another, you may be hurt. As Ann Kaiser Stearns writes, "Love is a lesson in vulnerability. It teaches us that we have no guarantee against having to give up the people and things most precious to us."

Dare to love again. God's love risked Jesus. When He gave Christ, He risked our response of accepting or rejecting Him. We can do no less; we must take the model God presented to us in Christ and love again.

After Catherine Marshall's husband Peter died, she

wrote the book *To Live Again.* It's a good book with a great title. I think, though, for many the decision is to *love* again.

When you're in the midst of deep emotional pain, "God loves you" may seem like an irrelevant platitude, but I've known scores of people who wouldn't have made it had it not been for the knowledge of God's love for them. Only the love of God is eternal, unshakeable, unchanging. Paul put it so eloquently:

> *For I am certain that nothing can separate us from his love: neither death nor life, neither angels nor other heavenly rulers or powers, neither the present, nor the future, neither the world above nor the world below—there is nothing in all creation that will ever be able to separate us from the love of God which is ours through Christ Jesus our Lord.*
>
> Romans 8:38, 39 TEV

The knowledge that this unconditional love is yours for the taking can sustain you in the midst of experiencing rejection and the loss of someone you love.

Many psychologists suggest that the major obstacle in adapting to the loss of a loved one stems from the fear that somehow something is wrong with us, that we are no longer worthy or desirable. It's much like abused children who feel they're to blame for their being abused. One of the causes of these kinds of feelings is a lack of self-worth, the feeling that we're not valued by anyone.

Some time ago I read a new interpretation of God's loving and watchful care for His children. It said: "You're so beautiful in God's sight that He can't take His eyes off of you." Every person is beautiful in God's sight. Every person is loved and of great worth to God. Remember, you're a creation of God the Father and a child of the King. And, as His child, you're accepted and loved.

The cellist Pablo Casals remarked, "The main thing in life is not to be afraid to be human." Those who go through life afraid to love, afraid to commit for fear that love will go away, will never fully realize their human potential. You cannot withhold your own love and expect to receive love from another.

> *Give to others, and God will give to you. Indeed, you will receive a full measure, a generous helping, poured into your hands—all that you can hold. The measure you use for others is the one that God will use for you.*
>
> Luke 6:38 TEV

LESSONS FROM THE TREES

External support

Supplying artificial support to injured and flawed trees has long been recognized as an important part of their recovery. Some trees have inherent structural weakness resulting from the manner in which their branches arise. To survive, they often require considerable mechanical bracing. It's an inexpensive form of tree insurance which prevents injuries and prolongs the life of the tree.

People, too, sometimes need external bracing. In divorce, especially, many people genuinely need the strong support of others. The solemn vow to stay together "until death us do part" has been broken. The end of the marriage is like a form of living death to many. In fact, the trauma from divorce may cause some to need support more than at any other time in their lives.

That's when the support of loved ones, friends, and church members becomes so crucial. That's when God uses others to be His bearers of sensitive and understanding love. It can be a simple form of reassurance that until the weakened person can stand alone, he or she will be propped up and supported by those who love and care for them.

Especially important is the recognition of the *invisible* presence and support of the Holy Spirit. When added to the *visible* support of the church, His presence becomes life-sustaining for us in our times of great need.

5

Losing a
Loved One:

How grief can heal
your pain

A man once talked with God, saying, "Lord, as I've walked along life's path, many times I've looked back and have seen two sets of footprints in the sand, and I knew that one set was Yours. But, lately, when I've needed You most, when things have been the most difficult, I've looked back and have only seen one set of footprints."

God answered him gently, "That's because those were the times when I carried you. The single set of prints you've seen were Mine."

In my ministry of feeding hungry children around the world, I've traveled to many countries and foreign lands. In nearly all of them, I find some kind of calamity. Many times, it's due to natural causes such as famine, flood, or earthquake. Other times, it's man's own inhumanity to man.

In Central America, the problem is not caused by nature. In fact, this is a beautiful area that could be self-sustaining were it not for the conflict among the people. In my travels, I've visited the capitals of Honduras, Guatemala, Nicaragua, El Salvador, Costa Rica, Belize, and Panama. In each place, I discovered a reality that keeps hitting me like a sledgehammer every time I visit. These people live with death every day. They see it in their towns and villages; they see it when it happens to their neighbors; and they also see it when it happens in their own families.

In Nicaragua, one morning at dawn, six soldiers came to the home of Jorges and Maria. They dragged Jorges out of the house and as his family watched helplessly, they murdered him in cold blood. Then, in full view of the family, they raped Maria. Afterwards, as the family fled to Costa Rica, one of the six children died, another was stolen and sold.

I met Maria while I was in Costa Rica distributing food to refugee children from the area. The morning I visited with her, her children were in a nearby town, begging for bread. As she told me her story, she cried out, full of anguish and bitterness, "My heart will not stop weeping." She was bent as far as she could go, almost ready to break.

Naturally, when I heard her story, I was outraged. Men who hide behind uniforms to commit murder and rape do not deserve to walk around free. Yet it had happened, and the family was suffering the bitter consequences. If ever a person had a right to be bitter, Maria did!

What could I do? There was no way I could right the many wrongs that she had suffered. The fighting, the revolutions and wars were not in my power to solve. Although I was able to provide a significant amount of food for her family, I couldn't bring her dead husband back. I couldn't restore her baby boy to life. I had no idea where her daughter had been taken, and I couldn't remove the sense of shame she felt at being violated in front of her children.

But there was one thing very clear to me about Maria's grief: it was costing too much for Maria to be bitter, because it was destroying her will to live and what little strength she had left. The death of her husband and her baby were almost more than she could take.

As any of us who have experienced the loss of a loved one know, there's nothing so painful and so final as death. And when it's brutal and unexpected, as was the case for Maria, the pain is even more intense. Even when it's expected, when it may mean the end of suffering, it's still not easy. The reality that the one who has died will never be present again in this life is often a bitter, bitter experience. That's when the message of eternal life through Christ becomes so special, so precious. To those for whom death is so pervasive, the comfort of knowing that they will one day see their loved ones again is their most important assurance. And yet that does not make the feeling of loss go away.

I know of a pastor and his wife who lost a baby many years ago while attending a summer camp meeting. The baby took a turn for the worse so quickly that before they realized it and called the doctor, it was too late. They were young Christians and they listened to elders who advised them to stay at the campsite and have the funeral there. The featured camp speaker gave the sermon. Looking at the young, bereaved couple, he said, "Excessive grief is unchristian." Not wanting to appear "unchristian," the couple stifled their grief, holding back the sobs of unconsoled sorrow that racked their hearts.

It was only much later in life that they realized how wrong the speaker had been. It was many years later before they felt free to mention their baby's name, to cry, to say how cute he was, how missed he was. They had missed out on one of the most important ways God ministers healing to us.

1. Grieving is God's way of healing our loss.

Jesus went to the home of Mary and Martha on hearing of the death of their brother. There, according to Scripture, is the only time "Jesus wept." (*See* John 11:35, 36.) There is absolutely nothing wrong with grieving. We shouldn't cut it short, ignore it, or hope it will go away. Grief is real and must be experienced. Who's to say what "excessive grief" is?

More importantly, God grieves with us at our loss. If God sees the sparrow fall, then He feels our pain and hurt. Moreover, if we deny our pain and hurt, if we fail to express our grief, then we deny it to God as well. There's nothing more important for us when grieving than to express our grief to God. Others understand, but God knows what we're going through like no one else possibly could. He truly understands. With God, we can say anything, express any feeling, release any feeling. God will understand.

More so than with any other experience, we wish grief to end and pain to expire. We want to push the "fast forward" button of life and have our grief over with quickly. But someone who has been a significant part of our lives will always remain an equally significant part of our memories. That's what grief really is: dealing with the change between what once was and what now is.

2. Give yourself a time frame for your grief.

In the wisdom of the book of Ecclesiastes, it says, "To every thing there is a season, and a time to every purpose under the heaven . . . a time to weep" (3:1, 4). There is a time to weep—when grieving is appropriate and called for. But then, there's also a time when grieving and weeping should cease.

That doesn't mean you are never to grieve again, but it does mean that you cannot let your whole day be consumed by grieving. Life does go on. We have to fulfill responsibilities to ourselves and to others. That means we may need a specific "grief time." In other words, we may need a specific time of the day or evening when we grieve over our loss. Until that time of the day, we will commit to ourselves that we will push it out of our minds and hearts until our appointed "grief time."

In the same way that wounds of trees are healed by natural processes, so God uses the natural grieving processes to heal our loss and to help us overcome our bitterness. The bitterness can be erased. The pain can be relieved. In time, God heals all.

3. Make it through this minute.

Colonel Robinson Risner, one of America's P.O.W.s during the Vietnam War, was imprisoned for more than seven and a half years. Because he was a leader, and because of his indomitable faith and courage, he was tortured beyond belief. One of the ways that he relates how he made it was living only sixty seconds at a time. When the pain was at its worst, he would repeat to himself over and over, "I can take anything for sixty seconds." Again and again, he fought—minute by minute, hour by hour. The days passed and the years came and went, and finally, one day he was back home again.

There are times when pain is unbearable, when nothing and no one seems to help. In those times we can only cling to the moment, knowing that God will see us through the next sixty seconds. Philippians 4:13 says, "I can do all things through Christ which strengtheneth me." That is not only a scriptural promise, it's also a living reality. We can make it through our grief "through Christ which strengtheneth me."

4. Find help through caring friends.

It's important to know when we experience a death in our family that we are not alone. Others have experienced the death of their loved ones, too. Helen Keller movingly described this lesson. She said, "We bereaved are not alone. We belong to the largest company in all the world—the company of those who have known suffering. When it seems that our sorrow is too great to be borne, let us think of the great family of the heavy-hearted into which our grief has given us entrance, and inevitably, we will feel about us their arms, their sympathy, their understanding."

My wife, Frances, wrote a very moving book on the loss of her father. We submitted it to more than ten publishers. Each said it was a well-written and worthy effort; yet, none was willing to publish it. Their response was that they simply didn't think people wanted to read books about death. So we published it ourselves. We learned that most people are not prepared for death and don't know how to handle their grief. Their loss breaks them so that they no longer want to live; they have little or no concern for any loved ones they have left. They simply cannot accept the death of one they loved so much. Many people have written to Frances to tell her how helpful that book has been. They said things like, "It helped to know someone else had been through the same problems. It helped to know that you made it. That means I can make it, too."

Carl Jung, the noted Austrian therapist, once said that, "Only the wounded doctor can heal." Those who've lost a loved one themselves know the pain that others are experiencing. Those who have been stricken with grief know how immobilizing it can be. And Helen Keller said:

> *Robbed of joy, of courage, of the very desire to live, the newly bereaved frequently avoids companionship, feeling themselves so limp with misery and so empty of vitality that they are ill-suited for human contacts. And yet no one is so bereaved, so miserable, that they cannot find someone else to succor, someone who needs friendship, understanding, and courage more than they. The unselfish effort to bring cheer to others will be the beginning of a happier life for ourselves.*

During the early part of the 1980s, I made many trips to Ethiopia to help relieve some of the massive starvation that country was experiencing. I still am reeling from the impact of the deaths I saw: little children dying in their mothers' arms; doctors without enough medicine or helpers; mothers and fathers dying where they sat. It was awful. Life seemed so terribly cheap. And yet it was no less real because of the numbers of people dying. Parents still hurt; children still cried; and death was no less weakened by it all. As I would minister to them, their eyes would fill with tears, and sometimes I cried with them. The interpreters would tell me what they were saying, and I would do the best I could to let them know that I cared, that I understood, and that God would see them through this nightmare. At night, however, when I tried to sleep, the images of those babies and their mothers and fathers would not go away. I would begin to think, "What if I'd brought

63

more medicine or sent more doctors? What if the hundreds of farmer friends I have knew about this? What if . . . what if . . ." That was another way of saying, "If only I had done more, there wouldn't have been so many to die." I felt responsible for these people dying!

Many times, I'm told, one of the most difficult aspects of dealing with the passing of a loved one is our feeling of responsibility for their passing. We think if only we had done something differently . . . if only we had not said what we said . . . if only we had been more aware. On and on the list grows. If not curbed, *if only* can grow and grow until it becomes totally disproportionate to the reality of the situation.

Mary and Martha were this way even with Jesus. They said to Him when He arrived upon hearing of the death of their brother, "If only You had been here, our brother would not have died." The clear charge was that their brother's death was Jesus' fault.

I truly believe *if only* will make us miss out on the comfort and healing that can come from the good memories of our loved ones who have gone on before us. Faith says, "I loved them when they were alive and I'll treasure their memory forever"—not "If only I had done differently they would be alive." Faith says, "Their life was in God's hands and He saw fit to let them go"—not "Their life was in my hands and I let them go." *If only* is a lie without truth or foundation. Our lives are in God's hands as are our deaths. He controls the past, the present, and the future. He decides when and how. We're not the deciders of who lives and who dies.

As I struggled in Ethiopia, I finally realized that I was doing all I could do. That when I did the best I could, I had to leave everything else to God. And so, I comforted each one as best I could. I prayed. I listened. I was there as a friend, an ambassador of Christ. And it seemed to help them. Though it didn't stop the dying, though it didn't relieve their grief, it did mean there were others who cared, who were concerned, and who were there.

5. Our greatest consolation is the hope we have in Christ of the Resurrection.

Just after Russia's Communist Revolution, an attempt was made to destroy the Russian peasants' faith in Christianity. For that purpose there was formed "The Atheistic Society of the Militant Godless." This group would send lecturers all over Russia to convince the illiterate peasants that religion had no place in the new scientific order.

During its campaign, one of the most brilliant lecturers was sent to a particular town. Officials had assembled a thousand farmers and workers into a big hall. For more than an hour the scientist harangued the people, declaring that Christianity was the "narcotic of the capitalists," an "opiate" used to deny the peasants their rights. As he ridiculed the Christian faith and insulted Christ (he even tore up the pages of the Bible) the peasants sat motionless and afraid. They were defeated. Soldiers were everywhere. They had no power. Many hung their heads, ashamed of their inability to fight back.

Finally, the lecturer, convinced that his brilliant arguments had discredited the faith which had long been in Russia, said, "Now, do any of you have any questions?"

Not a person raised a hand. The silence of defeat became deafening.

But, as the lecturer looked down the hall, there, coming up the side aisle, was an old man with white hair and beard, wearing a typical long Russian coat and high boots. He moved toward the platform with a deliberate, determined stride, each step resounding through the hall.

When he reached the platform, the old man was asked, "Well, what is your question?" Scorning the lecturer with silence, the man turned toward the audience and raising his arms very slowly toward heaven, he shouted the greeting which for centuries Russian peasants have given each other on Easter morning, *"Christos Vrookress!"* Christ is Risen! Suddenly, as the old man shouted this wondrous greeting, a thousand peasants jumped to their feet and shouted back until the hall shook with the thunder of their exclamation, *"Christos Voskinin!"* Christ is Risen, indeed!

At times, grief can cause us to bow our heads in resignation, believing that all we have to look forward to is more pain and grief. But, let's not forget the hope of the Resurrection. Because Christ is risen, we can claim the promise of new life. Death is not a period, but a comma that precedes a deeper life. It's the anesthetic of the Great Physician opening the door to an eternal life with Christ. It's the last enemy we face, and "thanks be to God who giveth us the victory through our Lord Jesus Christ" over that enemy.

I have to confess that I don't read much poetry. However, recently, a friend shared with me one of Henry Wadsworth Longfellow's poems. Longfellow wrote it three years after the death of his young wife. It is the very best poem on death I've ever read. It ministered to me and my prayer is that it will minister to you as well.

> *Tell me not, in mournful numbers,*
> *Life is but an empty dream!*
> *For the soul is dead that slumbers,*
> *And things are not what they seem.*
>
> *Life is real! Life is earnest!*
> *And the grave is not its goal;*
> *Dust thou art, to dust returnest,*
> *Was not spoken of the soul.*
>
> *Not enjoyment, and not sorrow,*
> *Is our destined end or way;*
> *But to act, that each tomorrow*
> *Find us farther than today.*
>
> *Art is long, and Time is fleeting,*
> *And our hearts, though stout and brave,*
> *Still, like muffled drums, are beating*
> *Funeral marches to the grave.*
>
> *In the world's broad field to battle,*
> *In the bivouac of Life,*
> *Be not like dumb, driven cattle!*
> *Be a hero in the strife!*
>
> *Trust no Future, howe'er pleasant!*
> *Let the dead Past bury its dead!*
> *Act,—act in the living Present!*
> *Heart within, and God o'erhead!*
>
> *Lives of great men all remind us*
> *We can make our lives sublime,*
> *And, departing, leave behind us*
> *Footprints on the sand of time;*

Footprints, that perhaps another,
Sailing o'er life's solemn main,
A forlorn and shipwrecked brother,
Seeing, shall take heart again.

Let us then, be up and doing,
With a heart for any fate;
Still achieving, still pursuing,
Learn to labor and to wait.

LESSONS FROM THE TREES

Treatment of wounds

Once a tree has been pruned or a limb broken, the wound must heal or insects and disease will attack the weakened spot. Healing takes place by the formation of layers of callus tissue that form around the edge of the wound. The callus tissue growth averages about one-half inch in thickness each year. Consequently, the larger the wound, the longer it takes to heal.

Nature's way of healing is sometimes slow and tedious, but healing occurs nonetheless. This is an important fact to remember when we're suffering the pangs of grief and sorrow and wonder if we'll ever recover. Just as trees take time to recover from their wounds, so do people.

John 14 records one of the most moving statements of Jesus to His closest disciples. He knew that He would be leaving them; He knew the grief and the pain they would suffer; He knew the wound His departure would create. Cautiously and carefully, He told them what to expect. And He offered solace for the wounds they would have:

Let not your heart be troubled: ye believe in
God, believe also in me. In my Father's house
are many mansions: if it were not so, I would
have told you. I go to prepare a place for you.

> *And if I go and prepare a place for you, I will come again, and receive you unto myself; that where I am, there ye may be also.*

> John 14:1–3

He did leave; they did have sorrow over His departure; but He did prepare them for the wounds. If you're suffering from a significant loss, be aware of the time involved in the healing process. Accept the time it will take and lean on the One who can give you the hope and strength to hang on until you have recovered.

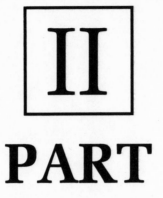

PART

Overcoming Adversity:

Finding relief from prolonged distress

6

Loneliness:

Removing your fear

"Give, and it will be given to you; good measure, pressed down, shaken together, running over.... For the measure you give will be the measure you get back."

Luke 6:38 RSV

Give a little of yourself to someone else, and you'll be surprised at the return you receive.

There's no loneliness like the loneliness of dying alone. There's no love greater than loving and caring for lonely, dying people. That's what Mother Teresa does; it's why the world has recognized her as a special person, worthy of the Nobel Prize.

I saw the colleagues of Mother Teresa working in the streets of Addis Ababa when the nation of Ethiopia was gripped with death and dying. Each morning, these "Missionaries of Charity" would make a sweep of the capital city. I watched with incredulous admiration as they combed the gutters and dumps for people who had absolutely no one. With an incredible kind of love, they would bend over and pick up one frail and dying body after another—men, women, and children who were dying from disease, starvation, and illness. Lovingly and gently, as if they were their own mothers or fathers, they carried them back to the hospice where they were cleaned up, given food if they were able to eat, and more than anything, given love and the dignity of dying where someone cared.

The transformation was miraculous. Their demeanor, their attitude, their energy changed incredibly. All because someone cared; because someone was willing to be present in their most lonely time. I joined these sisters as they made their journey. It wasn't easy. The smells were so strong that I can still remember them. But I saw the difference that the willingness to be present in someone else's moment of loneliness can make.

There are five billion people on the face of the earth. Untold millions of them are so utterly lonely—and it's not just in far-off places like Ethiopia, but right here in these United States of America. When my wife, Frances, and I distributed Mobile Meals, the recipients all looked forward to the food, but what they also were hungry for was the smile, the visit, someone to listen, a friendly face. They were so terribly lonely.

One of the reasons some people break under the pressure of modern living is a social development caused, at least in part, by what psychologists call "anonymity," or the feeling of having lost our identity. Many factors contribute to this feeling: the breakup of home and family; a mobile society which prevents our putting down roots; urbanization and the pattern of not even knowing your next-door neighbor; and the the disorienting pace of modern life.

Alvin Toffler, in his book, *Future Shock*, says human

beings can only adapt to a certain number of changes without suffering despair and a feeling of helplessness.

> *Despite its extraordinary achievements in art, science, intellectual, moral and political life, the United States is a nation in which tens of thousands of young people flee reality by opting for a drug-induced lassitude; a nation in which millions of their parents retreat into video-induced stupor or alcoholic haze; a nation in which legions of elderly folk vegetate and die in loneliness; in which masses tame their anxieties with Miltown, or Librium, or Equanil, or a score of other tranquilizers and psychic pacifiers.*

Everywhere I go, I sense this underlying feeling of loneliness, especially among young adults and the elderly. Millions of people now live alone, and that number is increasing. Young adults are postponing marriage and leaving home to create new households, often by themselves. And the fastest growing segment in our population is the over-eighty age group, many of whom live alone.

You may be feeling isolated and alone, your family members scattered, your daily contacts with people superficial and unfulfilling. You may not even know your next-door neighbor.

But, physical aloneness does not have to cause loneliness. Remember, you're a child of a God who says, "The very hairs of your head are all numbered" (Matthew 10:30). It is possible to overcome loneliness, *to bend and not break.*

1. Understand the cause of loneliness.

There are many different kinds of loneliness. The most serious is spiritual loneliness. Its cause is estrangement from God. That's why God sent Christ into the world to restore our relationship to Himself. When we receive Christ into our lives, our spiritual loneliness leaves. Truly, Christ is the "friend who sticketh closer than a brother." God sent Jesus into the world and the Word became flesh. That was the event of events—God became flesh. We never need to be lonely again when we have Christ.

Being alone can also create feelings of loneliness, but many people who live by themselves do not suffer from loneliness. Loneliness stems from an inner attitude about our circumstances. Loneliness is not the only possible feeling in such a situation. Even though we don't always have control over external circumstances, we do have control over our attitudes toward those circumstances.

As a former college athlete, I still keep up with a lot of college sports. I was stricken by the response of Fred Akers, the coach at the University of Texas, when he was fired after ten years. He said, "I didn't have a choice in whether I was fired, but I do have a choice as to how I react to that firing. I had a lot of good years here, and I have a lot of good years left. I will land on my feet." Although he had been fired from his job, they had not been able to destroy his positive attitude. That's why it's so important to commit to an overcoming attitude. As Oswald Chambers said, "God does not give us overcoming life. He gives us life as we overcome."

Examine your feelings of loneliness. When do you feel the most pain? What causes those feelings of isolation to flood your soul? What steps can you take toward accepting your own situation?

People who do not like themselves have trouble being alone. They need other people to affirm their worth; they look to others for their own identity. Look inside yourself. Like what you see. Are you someone you'd like for a best friend? If so, learn how to be your own "best friend."

2. Get involved with other people.

Someone has wisely said that we don't wait for others to feed us food when we're hungry. We prepare the food ourselves because we know it's vital to our survival. Yet, when we're hungry for companionship, we often sit by waiting for others to nourish and befriend us.

One of the most admirable persons I've ever known is Mrs. Kirtley, the widow of a minister. Mrs. Kirtley is in her eighties and constantly on the go. If you were to call her early on a Thursday morning, you'd discover that she was on her way "to visit the old people at the nursing home."

When I was in seminary, I rented a room from Mrs. Kirtley. Once a month, usually on a Tuesday at 10:00 P.M., she would invite me and the others renting rooms from her down to her room for milk and cookies. What I learned from her was that even though she lived alone, she made sure she wasn't lonely.

If you're feeling isolated and alone, pick up the telephone and call someone you know. Take the risk of being rejected; take the risk of making a new friend. You've got a 50-50 chance of changing your situation. If you don't have a friend you're willing to call on socially, volunteer your time to help a stranger through some social service organization. Whatever you do, give a little of yourself to someone else, and you'll be surprised at the return you receive.

Sometimes we can't see the light at the end of the tunnel. Every way we look seems to be dark and gloomy.

While we're searching for the light we can also help others who are in the tunnel with us. Though neither they nor you may know when or how you'll find the tunnel's end, together you can help each other, and in the process, the pain of loneliness will be assuaged. As Jesus said, "Give, and it shall be given unto you; good measure, pressed down, and shaken together, and running over, shall men give into your bosom. For with the same measure that ye mete withal it shall be measured to you again" (Luke 6:38).

3. Develop a daily time of prayer and meditation.

After we have accepted Christ, a time set aside each day for prayer and meditation will strengthen us inside greatly. I've discovered that if it's the first thing you do each day that it will set the pattern for the rest of the day. It's as though we choose to invite God to help us make that day's agenda.

When I was still in college and Frances and I were still dating, we would meet each morning at 8:00 before our 8:40 class for a devotional of prayer and Scripture. The devotional guide we used was by Bishop Ralph S. Cushman. One of the most helpful parts of his book was the following poem:

The Secret

I met God in the morning
When my day was at its best,
And his presence came like sunrise,
Like a glory in my breast.

All day long the Presence lingered,
All day long he stayed with me,
And we sailed in perfect calmness
O'er a very troubled sea.

> *Other ships were blown and battered,*
> *Other ships were sore distressed,*
> *But the winds that seemed to drive them*
> *Brought to us a peace and rest.*

> *Then I thought of other mornings,*
> *With a keen remorse of mind,*
> *When I too had loosed the moorings,*
> *With the Presence left behind.*

> *So I think I know the secret,*
> *Learned from many a troubled way:*
> *You must seek him in the morning*
> *If you want him through the day!*

Remember, Jesus said He would not leave us orphans but would send the Holy Spirit to comfort and be present with us.

It's important that we commit ourselves to praying, regardless of what happens. That's not easy and it's not something we do automatically. It has to become like brushing our teeth—almost second nature.

4. Look beyond loneliness to what God has ahead for you.

Sometimes the experience of a long, lonely day can blur our vision. We begin to see our total life through our "lonely" eyes. It becomes impossible to see through the storm we're experiencing to the light that will come sooner or later.

I remember being with my family in Clearwater, Florida, on vacation when a storm blew in. It began raining so hard that we pulled off the road because we could not see through the storm. We were uneasy and inconvenienced, yet we knew that the storm would subside sooner or later. We had to look ahead and look beyond the storm.

Loneliness is often only temporary. And through the pain of it all, the Lord is there to comfort and support you. He may not part the ocean as He did for Moses. He may not bring down the walls of Jericho as He did for Joshua. But, He will be that "Rock of Ages" that can sustain and keep you. He will enable you to *bend and not break.*

While in East Africa several years ago, I was traveling to an important meeting, when our vehicle passed by a group of very distraught women. Each one had an empty basket on her head. By the way they were acting, I knew something was terribly wrong. We were in a hurry, but we stopped anyway. When we did, I discovered something that was more important than my meeting: these women had been depending on one of their number catching the bus that morning to a distant water well. She would then have brought back water for the others. But the bus had been full that day and now they all faced an entire day and night without water.

On the spot, God had interrupted my plans. We used our vehicle to go and secure water. I talked with some of the men in the village and soon had a pretty good picture of the need. First, I arranged for a truck to haul water in to the village. Then, with the help of the Oak Ridge Boys back in America, we were able to build four wells for the village. One member of the quartet told me that the last time he was there he saw between 4,000 and 5,000 head of cattle drinking from *one* of the wells!

How glad I was that God interrupted my plans! The more I thought about it, the more I realized that most of Jesus' miracles happened when He was interrupted. Interruptions can be the way God chooses to ease and erase our loneliness. Maybe that needs to happen to you. Be open to God's giving you new direction for your life and changing the way you're headed.

LESSONS FROM THE TREES

The banyan tree

The banyan tree, a species of fig tree native to eastern India, is one of the wonders of the plant world. If necessary, its seed can germinate on other plants, which it then uses for support. It survives during this time by getting its sustenance from the air. Its roots grow down from high branches and after penetrating the ground, they increase in thickness, forming great pillars to support the branches. Thus, a single plant, which began without ground roots, can turn into a kind of forest a thousand feet across.

The banyan tree has a lesson to teach us about loneliness. Many people today feel isolated and alone. They look around for places to put down roots and don't find them. Yet, like the banyan tree, it's possible to find many places to be nurtured and to grow in the most unlikely places. The banyan tree survives because it adapts to its environment; its adaptation is one of nature's most marvelous feats.

If you're feeling alone, far from family and friends, look around for new ways to find support. It may be that you've been looking in only familiar places. Don't allow feelings of loneliness and isolation to keep you from exploring the new. You may be surprised at what you find. And in the process, put down new roots which will sustain you and enable you to meet the new problems that life poses.

Sickness:

Looking up when you're lying down

"I learned in the Nazi concentration camps during World War II that everything external can be taken from you. But the one thing no one can take away is how you choose to respond to what they've done. One's attitude is the last of the human freedoms."

DR. VIKTOR FRANKL

Stan Mooneyham, the Honorary Chairman of Feed the Children, has described his illness in this way:

There are days and there are nights when the only prayer I can pray is the one prayed by Middle East desert fathers back in the Third and Fourth Centuries: "Oh God, according to my great need and your abundant supply, please help me." It's the only prayer that means anything, the prayer that expresses the deepest feeling in my heart.

In 1984, after years of traveling all over the world in the service of suffering humanity, Stan Mooneyham developed an illness which literally knocked him off his feet. For days and weeks, he was too weak to work, and Stan had a great deal of difficulty accepting the tremendous changes this brought in his life-style.

> *At first I went into a denial stage. I mean, I've been the Sherman tank, plowing through the world, never recognizing illness, weakness, aging, or anything else. I thought I was indestructible, that I was going to live to be at least ninety-two or ninety-three, have good health right up to the last minute, and then drop over dead and go to heaven.*
>
> *Well, after a while I learned that denial does nothing but kid yourself, so I went into a stage I call reluctant acceptance. I acknowledged that the illness was happening to me, but it wasn't going to affect the way I lived.*
>
> *But, I soon discovered that wasn't so. Sometimes I had to carry a cane, and I began to understand what it must be like for accident victims to accept a wheelchair. What bitterness they must feel. So, I began to pray for God to cure me.*

When the cure did not come, Stan came to see that what he really needed was a deeper healing, not just a curing of the body, but a healing of the mind and spirit and the emotions that would include the acceptance of what was happening to him, the acknowledging and yielding to a reality he didn't want to accept.

As his illness continued and his understanding of living with the illness progressed, Stan began praying for the "right things," as he put it.

> *I had such few and rare good days that occasionally when I would have a good one, then the next day I would pray, "Lord, let me have a good day or at least give me the strength to function whether I feel good or not." And I*

discovered that I can function even when I don't feel good. That was a great breakthrough for me, a great revelation.

Yet, some days, I don't handle my illness well at all. I get angry and regress into a cycle of defeat. I still go back and forth in my own emotions and my own spirit. But, in my darkest moments, in those times when all other words are meaningless, I pray, "Oh, God! According to my great need, and according to your abundant supply, please help me."

At this writing, Stan's struggle with his illness is not over. Many of you may understand exactly what he faces every day because you, too, are living with a sickness that challenges your faith and your ability to cope with everyday living.

The other day I was talking with Stan on the phone and he told me of his struggle the previous Sunday. He had arisen feeling very sick, and yet he knew he had responsibilities in both services that morning at the church he attended. So he asked his wife, Nancy, to join him in praying for himself. Together, they prayed, "Lord, we believe Matthew 18:19, 'That if two of you shall agree on earth as touching any thing that they shall ask, it shall be done for them of my Father which is in heaven.' We two are agreeing this morning in prayer and asking you for functional grace this morning. Give me enough strength so that I can function and fulfill the responsibilities I have." He said after they prayed, he ate breakfast, got ready, left and went to church. And though he was weak, he *functioned*: he did what was expected. Afterwards he went home and went to bed. He said as he lay in bed, he gave God thanks for *functional grace*.

My own mother-in-law, Mrs. Effie Hackler, lived out her last days with us. My wife, Frances, had to live through incredible suffering and pain with her. It was not easy to see one who had been so vibrant and alive reduced to such an existence.

Despite all the medical advances we're making these days, sickness still comes. It robs us of our strength and vitality; it erodes our physical well-being, and it makes us terribly dependent on others. For most of us, it is not a question of *if* we will ever be sick, but *when*. Nearly all of us will at some time or another face a serious illness. How will we face it?

There's no situation where it is more important to think about our attitude than when we're sick. What I say stems in part from the experience of Viktor Frankl, who spent several years of his life in the concentration camps of Nazi Germany. Dr. Frankl, at the time of his imprisonment, was one of Vienna's most distinguished psychiatrists. He had a wife and family, prestige and success. And then the nightmare of Nazi Germany destroyed his career, his family, his future.

For reasons he was never able to understand, he was spared from immediate death. Instead, he was one of the thousands who performed slave labor. Day after day, in good weather and bad, they would be marched out to perform the most inhuman of tasks. At night, exhausted, they would trudge back to their camps.

In the midst of this pain and suffering, Dr. Frankl said he saw some of the most inspiring acts of human kindness that he had ever witnessed. In spite of the Nazi edict against prisoners helping each other, there were those who would still give away their last bit of food to someone starving. They would try to hide someone ill from the certain death that awaited them. They refused to let their attitudes sink to the level of their Nazi captors.

Dr. Frankl said that was when he made a tremendous discovery about life: our attitude is the last of the human freedoms. Despite the situation we may find ourselves in, our attitude is in our control. We can choose how we will respond to a given situation. Everything can be taken— even our health—and we still can refuse to let our attitude match the external events of our life.

A friend of mine who pastored in the south told me a remarkable story of Clara, a woman in his church. She truly understood the power of her own attitude. He said she was blind and one of her legs had been amputated. Yet, she was one of the most positive people he'd ever met. "I have a husband, my children, and a church that prays for me," she said. "I have every reason to be happy."

Then the pastor told me something else about Clara. "She doesn't want us to pray for her with a 'poor Clara' attitude," he explained. "So every time we get ready to pray for her during the church service, I hold up a horn in the air and honk it twice!"

Clara can't control her own physical situation, but she can determine how she and others relate to it. I certainly don't intend to minimize the seriousness of an illness. Severe sickness is not something to take lightly. When one is sick, it casts a pall on everything, and many times it's almost impossible to maintain a positive attitude. One of our former employees has cancer, and she told me recently that out of the seven people who took chemotherapy with her, five are now dead. She is fighting a severe bout of depression, and I can certainly understand why. However, the reality remains that our attitude toward our sickness is a powerful weapon.

One of the most impressive pieces of work that's been done in this area comes from Norman Cousins, onetime editor of *The Saturday Review*. Dr. Cousins became seriously ill at the height of his career and was given a very negative prognosis by his physicians. He was told to prepare for a great deal of pain and medication, and to get ready to die.

But there was something in Dr. Cousins that would not accept that. He began working hard at changing his attitude about his sickness, to attack it mentally and emotionally, to work at laughing and being positive. The miracle of it all was that his attidude, along with the advice of his physician, worked. Cousins had a remission of his illness and has since gone on to do a significant amount of work and research on the relationship between attitude and sickness.

I don't mean to say that all you need to do to be well is to change your attitude. But one thing that will help you deal with your sickness is to change your attitude about it.

1. Know that God does not will sickness upon us.

Jesus said, "I am come that they might have life, and that they might have it more abundantly" (John 10:10). It's a fraudulent theology that tries to twist and distort faith to make us think that God has visited sickness upon us. God is *for* us. God doesn't will sickness; God is a good God. When we suffer pain and sickness, God suffers pain and sickness. Whatever we feel, God feels, because God is in us through Christ. Seventy percent of the ministry of Jesus as related in the New Testament was in the area of physical healing. Jesus was concerned about health both when He was on earth and now that He's in heaven.

When we're sick, it seems as if death is closer than ever.

I've always thought sickness was what David was refer-
ring to in the Twenty-Third Psalm when he said, "Yea,
though I walk through the valley of the *shadow* of death."
Sickness is like the shadow of death. But it's just that—
the shadow, not the real thing. And in the shadow of
death, God is with us. He is not the cause of our sickness,
but the One present with us in our sickness when we
walk through the valley of the shadow of death. Third
John 2 states, "Beloved, I wish above all things that thou
mayest prosper and be in health, even as thy soul pros-
pereth." Health is God's will for us, not sickness.

2. Practice the presence of God.

What this means is to intentionally do those things that
draw us into communion with God. Prayer is one of the
most important things a sick person can do. Telling God
about our need and our pain is critical. In so doing, God
helps us to find a way to deal with the pain of that
moment. When there's no one else . . . when there are no
other resources . . . when there's no one and nobody to
turn to . . . God is always there.

I remember falling and bloodying my knees when I was
just a small boy. My mother knelt down and looked at my
knees and then picked me up and put me on her lap. She
said, "Larry, it's going to be okay, because Mother loves
you." It immediately felt better! You and I know that a
Mother's love doesn't do away with the bleeding or the
pain. Yet the awareness of her care and concern was
healing in itself.

In Romans 8:35–39, some of the most magnificent
words in the New Testament occur as the Apostle Paul
describes the encompassing power of the love of Christ.
He writes:

*Who shall separate us from the love of Christ?
shall tribulation, or distress, or persecution, or
famine, or nakedness, or peril, or sword? As it is
written, For thy sake we are killed all the day
long; we are accounted as sheep for the slaugh-
ter. Nay, in all these things we are more than
conquerors through him that loved us. For I am
persuaded, that neither death, nor life, nor
angels, nor principalities, nor powers, nor
things present, nor things to come, Nor height,
nor depth, nor any other creature, shall be able
to separate us from the love of God, which is in
Christ Jesus our Lord.*

We can practice God's presence because He is always
present within to help us, to strengthen us, to see us
through our darkest night.

3. When you're down, look up.

When our bodies get down, our attitudes can get us
down, too. Strangely, there seems to be a connection
between our attitudes and our illnesses. A good attitude
helps us get well quicker; a healthy body makes it easier
to have a good attitude. Each can be helpful to the other.
In fact, I continue to marvel every day of my life at the
miracle of the human body. They're marvelous instru-
ments. They're designed to last 120 years, according to
Dr. Kenneth Cooper, the famed fitness expert. The stories
of remission and restoration that have resulted from
persons who've worked to restore their bodies and to
maintain a positive attitude in the face of overwhelming
circumstances are incredible.

Sometime back I contracted a viral infection that
wouldn't go away. I kept on working until I became so
weak that I had either to go to the hospital or to the

doctor. When my doctor examined me, he gave me some disturbing news. He said not only did I have a viral infection, but there was no cure for it. When I explained that I had too much to do to stop, his response was, "You have no choice. You have to get more rest. That's the only thing that will help you get better. We can relieve the distress it's causing, but that won't cure it; rest is the only thing that will help finally."

What that meant was that in addition to going to bed early and getting a good night's rest, I also had to stop in the middle of the day and rest for two hours. Taking two hours out of the middle of the day was like throwing me in jail for two hours. I hated the idea of it. To be busy and active all day and then having to stop and lie down for two hours seemed like a great waste. Surely there was some pill or some injection that could do equally well.

I knew, though, that the doctor had my best interest at heart and that he knew far more about medicine than I did. So each day in the middle of the afternoon, I would lie flat on my back and rest for two hours without interruption. And each time I repeated to myself, "Lord, You said in Scripture, 'All things work together for good to them that love the Lord.' Help me discover the good in this experience."

And I did just that. In fact, I made some marvelous discoveries while on my back in bed lying down. One of the most significant was for me to realize that while I was lying flat on my back, I was also looking up. I took that to mean that my rest time could be a time to communicate with God in an unhurried, restful sense. Those two hours became some of the richest times I've ever had in communicating with God, in drawing close to God. I doubt if in all my busyness, I would ever have taken the time to center my life in tune with God's call and purpose had it not been for those two hours each day.

Out of that experience I committed to read ten chapters of the Bible each day for the rest of my life. That alone has been one of the most rewarding investments I've ever made. Now my spirit is thirsty each day waiting for the water of life in the Word.

I learned that truly all things work together for good to them that love the Lord. By working intentionally to keep a positive attitude, I was able to break new ground in spiritual development which I would not trade for anything.

Later, a dear friend of my ministry sent me a cassette tape which had a prayer on it. Since I was sick, my wife, Frances, listened to it for me. Even though I was feeling bad, I had made a commitment to preach a crusade in Kansas. As I prepared to leave, Frances kissed me goodbye and then said, "Here's something I want you to listen to tonight before you go to bed."

That night just before I turned off the light, I turned on the tape. It had more than an hour's message from this special friend, which I heard not only with my ears, but with my heart. There were a lot of Scripture passages and then at the end a prayer for my healing. The next morning when I awoke, a load had been lifted: I was healed. The time for my resting was over.

Today, as I think back on that time and the things that happened to me, I view it as one of the most significant times in my entire spiritual life. And the key was the attitude I was able to maintain. It was a point in my life that refreshed my whole ministry.

In Lillian Watson's book *Light from Many Lamps*, there's a story about the journalist, biographer, and historian Ray Stannard Baker. He lay on his hospital bed in agony and pain, the aftermath of a serious operation. He wondered, as the pain relentlessly stayed with him hour after hour, whether he would ever be well enough to resume his life's work. Most of the long night he lay awake, suffering intensely.

> Toward morning, he reached for the little red-bound book on the table beside him, the beloved copy of Marcus Aurelius' Meditations. He turned to a page he had marked and underscored:
>
> "In every pain let this thought be present, that there is no dishonor in it, nor does it make the governing intelligence worse.
>
> "Indeed, in the case of most pains, let this remark of Epicurus aid thee, that pain is neither intolerable nor everlasting—if thou bearest in mind that it has its limits, and if thou addest nothing to it in imagination.
>
> "It is in the power of the soul to maintain its own serenity and tranquility, and not to think that pain is an evil.
>
> "It will suffice thee to remember as concerning pain . . . that the mind may be stopping all manner of commerce and sympathy with the body, still retain its own tranquility."

As Ray reflected upon it, he remembered that W. H. Hudson wrote one of his best books, *Far Away from Long Ago*, while ill in bed; Robert Louis Stevenson wrote *Treasure Island* while suffering from tuberculosis. It dawned on him that Ray Baker could go on with his work, even there in the hospital—in spite of the pain.

Tranquility does not come easy when you are suffering, and it may not be possible to achieve control of an illness. But, the illness does not have to become who you are. In spite of the limitations that sickness puts on you, you are still a child of God, a human being with worth, someone to love and be loved. Accepting this is one of the ways you can *bend and not break* when sickness threatens your body and bitterness threatens your soul.

Finally, I'd like to suggest that you take a security check of your mind. Ask yourself these questions:

1. Do you know that God does not will us to be sick?

2. Do you know that all things work together for good to them that love the Lord?

3. Do you know that your spiritual attitude is an important part of both your spiritual and physical well-being?

4. Are you looking up on the inside even though your body is lying down?

If you had to answer *no* to any of these, go back and read this chapter again and then reconsider the question. And when you do, my prayer is that God will be present with you as never before.

LESSONS FROM THE TREES

The oak

> Live thy Life,
> Young and old,
> · Like yon oak,
> Bright in spring
> Living gold
>
> Summer-rich
> Then; and then

> *Autumn-changed*
> *Soberer-hued*
> *Gold again*
>
> *All his leaves,*
> *Fall'n at length,*
> *Look, he stands,*
> *Trunk and bough,*
> *Naked strength.*
>> ALFRED, LORD TENNYSON

The oak tree has been a symbol of strength used by poets and writers throughout the ages. Literature is filled with stories and poems describing the beauty of the oak tree. In the well-known poem above, Tennyson romanticizes the changes that the oak tree experiences as it passes from season to season.

Notice in particular the last line. When all the leaves have gone, and the oak stands alone, Tennyson says, the oak stands with "naked strength."

Sickness may have stripped you of emotional and physical strength. You may feel that everything you once were or could have been is gone. Take a lesson from the oak tree. Robbed of health, you can still stand with "naked strength."

In 2 Corinthians 12:9,10, Paul writes of God's encouragement to him as he prayed for the thorn in his flesh to be removed:

> *And he said unto me, My grace is sufficient for thee: for my strength is made perfect in weakness. Most gladly therefore will I rather glory in my infirmities, that the power of Christ may rest upon me. Therefore I take pleasure in infirmities, in reproaches, in necessities, in persecutions, in distresses for Christ's sake: for when I am weak, then am I strong.*

Nothing lasts forever. That's especially good to know when we're in pain or experiencing sickness. And whatever the future holds, we know that God will give us the strength and courage to face the changes that may come our way.

Starting a new phase
of living

"You may have a fresh start any moment you choose."

MARY PICKFORD

Aminister among textile mill people tells a story about making a call on an elderly member of his congregation. A neighbor had called to inform the pastor that Mrs. Gibson seemed to be under great stress, almost in a confused state. After climbing three flights of stairs in the tenement house, the minister knocked on the door. There was no answer. He knocked louder . . . still no response. As he started to leave, he heard the sound of sobbing. He turned around, pushed open the un-locked door, and followed the sounds to her small, dingy kitchen.

There on the floor he saw the crumpled shape of Mrs. Gibson, a totally distraught woman. Between sobs, she told her pastor, "No one really cares anymore. No one really cares."

Earlier that morning, she had made a trip to the welfare office. The people were busy. They seemed cold and impersonal. "They don't even know my name," she said between sobs. "All they want to know is my Social Security number. No one cares who I am. I'm just a number."

In America's youth-oriented culture, growing old is not something to look forward to. Contrasted with other cultures, ours does not revere age; in fact, we often shun the elderly, almost as if to ward off our own aging process. "Old age is the most unexpected of all the things that happen to a man," Leon Trotsky wrote. Even the psalmist suffered from the anxieties of aging, "Cast me not off in the time of old age," he wrote in Psalm 71:9. "Forsake me not when my strength faileth."

Psychologists suggest that the disappointments of old age are connected with an unwillingness to accept death. In other words, we bemoan the loss of a future. David Brandt writes in his book *Is That All There Is?*, "From the vantage point of old age, looking back at the roads not taken, the opportunities missed, the failures of nerve, the chance losses, it is easy to focus on what might have been and live with regret."

The failure to leave one's mark on the world—to be forgotten—is the oldest of fears, Brandt continues. In one way or another, it's the loss of a future. Some people are afraid they will not be remembered; others say they haven't done all they wanted to do, and others shrug their shoulders and ask, "Is that all there is?" However we approach the aging process, most people (myself included) find it extremely frustrating.

Retirement homes are filled with people who spend a lot of time living in a romanticized view of the past and being very fearful about the future. They often have numerous complaints and grudges—many of which center on the infrequency of visits from family members or friends. They are likely to be preoccupied with physical complaints and the temptation to feel sorry for themselves. Their feelings of helplessness and loneliness contribute to an outlook on life that is frequently despairing and hopeless.

Our nursing homes are most often dismal, depressing places filled with sights and smells that only serve to reinforce the mistaken belief that old age, as William Butler Yeats puts it, "is nothing but a tattered coat upon a stick."

As people begin to live longer, the aging process affects the entire family structure. One nursing home advertisement shows a daughter taking her mother to a nursing center because she can no longer care for her. As she leaves, the daughter turns to the camera and says, "It's the hardest thing I've ever done." In most families, both spouses work to maintain their standard of living, and when elderly parents need nursing care, no one is at home to care for them. It's a catch-22 situation. The children feel guilty, and the elderly parents feel abandoned.

Many of our country's poorest are elderly women, left alone to survive on the minimum benefits of Social Security, which, in today's economy, simply aren't enough. Add health problems, loneliness, and isolation to the whole aging process, and you can easily see why we all have some dread of growing old, and why some people become very bitter in the sunset of their lives.

John and Justina Balzar had every right to feel bitter. They were very happy living on the farm that had been home in Hooker, Oklahoma, for forty-four years. Then Justina suffered a stroke. John stepped in and took care of everything, nursing and caring for Justina, until he, too, was felled by a stroke. Then, like so many elderly, unable to care for themselves, they were forced to leave familiar surroundings and move into a retirement center in Kansas where they both could receive regular medical care.

Many people would have decided to give up on life at this point. But not John Balzar. He simply looked around to find something useful to do, and he found it. "When I quit farming, I thought I had to do something," he said. "Our kids told us, 'Don't just sit around and do nothing.' So I started to carve."

John had never carved anything in his life until that point. Today, twenty years later, John's works are on display in museums throughout North America, including the Smithsonian Institution, and he's won countless ribbons and awards for his work. Feed the Children has also benefited from his talent—several pieces have been sold and the proceeds used to help feed hungry children. All this from a man eighty-seven years old! He's not worried about his graying hair or even about his diminished physical strength. "I just pray for the Lord to be gracious to me and keep my mind clear as long as I live so that I can do something worthwhile for other people," John says. John wanted his life to count for something, so he found a way to continue contributing in spite of his health and age handicaps. It's a secret that has softened the hard edges that come with growing old.

What is it that allows a person like John Balzar to live out his years with such a positive attitude while others become defeated by the ravages of time that Mother Nature inevitably gives to us all? Colonel Sanders, the founder of the Kentucky Fried Chicken franchises, started his incredibly successful business *after* he had retired at age sixty-five and found himself feeling totally useless and defeated, wondering if life were really over for him. You know the rest of that story!

"To grow older is a new venture in itself," Goethe

wrote many years ago. Slowly but surely we're believing that statement. As the percentage of elderly in our population increases, finding ways to benefit from an increasingly older society will become important to all of us. In 1985, one out of four Americans was over the age of fifty. By the turn of the century, more than 100,000 Americans will be a hundred years old, or older, about three times the number today. By the year 2025, sixty-four million Americans will be over age sixty-five. We're headed toward a time when simply by strength of numbers the elderly will command respect and attention. We'll discover if "Age, cunning, and deceit can defeat youth, skill, and agility," as the comical T-shirt quote says.

But right now, we're in a period of transition, and many older people are bitter about the role they've been assigned. I believe that we can defeat the uncertainties and problems that most certainly accompany growing older. I believe it because I've seen so many inspiring examples of people who have done it. "You are never beaten unless you give up," the actress Mary Pickford said. "You may have a fresh start any moment you choose."

It is possible to *bend and not break* under the pressures and disillusionments of growing older.

1. Accept your age as the blessing of God.

It's important to stay in tune with the rhythm of aging that nature has for us. There's nothing more sad than watching someone trying to act either older or younger than they are. Haven't you seen a woman, too old to wear the trendy styles of her youth, still trying to dress as if she were a teenager? Or men who brag about physical feats they accomplished years ago, not willing to admit that those times are past? This doesn't mean that you have to look and act old. It simply means that as your body changes, you should accept those changes and not deny their existence.

When you're willing to accept your age, you no longer fight losing battles with yourself. You may not be able to run three miles around a track, but you can walk three miles. Why allow bitterness to defeat you when acceptance of change can give you peace?

2. Enjoy the benefits of aging.

Every age can have positive benefits if we can develop the ability to accept those benefits. Marcus Cicero described old age as the "crown of life, our play's last act." And, in the novel *Wrinkles*, Charles Simmons says about one of his characters, "Now he will be able to do whatever he wants with his time, civilization and nature having lost interest in him." Well, I'm not sure that it's a benefit to have someone lose interest in us, but as we grow older, some people do allow us a few more peculiarities!

Stan Mooneyham, long-time president of World Vision and now Honorary Chairman of Feed the Children, described how relieved he was, at age sixty-one, to be free to serve as "elder statesman" to younger men working in humanitarian causes. "For so long I worked in the trenches, competing, driving myself, thinking I had to do it all. Now, I can sit back and support others, and I feel good about this new role."

When the future begins to look dimmer, when you know that you have more years behind you than ahead, don't allow bitterness to invade your heart and soul. Think about the legacy you will leave and utilize all your energies to enhance that gift. "When I think of those who will come after—or survive me—I feel as if I were taking part in the preparations for a feast, the joys of which I shall not share," Dag Hammarskjold wrote so poetically in his book *Markings*.

3. Forgive the past.

Surely the sunset of life is the time to quit carrying grudges and old wounds and allow ourselves to carry a lighter load. My father-in-law, on his deathbed, had a great need to see two of his close relatives resolve their differences so he could die in peace.

With tears in his eyes, he called the two men to his side. Clasping their hands together across his bed, he pleaded with them to "bury the hatchet" and become friends again. In an emotional embrace, they asked for forgiveness, and a calm and peaceful atmosphere enveloped the room.

Mistakes from the past can make life's last years miserable. Worrying about what might have been can cloud an already dim present. "I only regret, in my chilled age, certain occasions and possibilities I didn't embrace," Henry James wrote in a letter to a friend about 1913.

As the book of Hebrews exhorts us, "Wherefore seeing we also are compassed about with so great a cloud of witnesses, let us lay aside every weight, and the sin which doth so easily beset us, and let us run with patience the race that is set before us" (Hebrews 12:1).

4. Keep on living.

One of the saddest things I know is to see someone who has given up on life, regardless of his or her age. "The ultimate evil is to leave the company of the living before you die," an old saying goes. Don't allow diminished capacities to defeat you. You can still learn new things, enjoy new experiences, and reap the harvest of memories and blessings stored up from your long years of living.

It's frustrating not to be able to do the things that once came so easily. "I don't remember growing old," a woman told me who had turned to alcohol to relieve the bitterness she was feeling about the aging process. "One day I was young; the next I was old. I don't know what happened in between."

"I'm glad to be old," one man remarked jokingly. "I don't like the alternative." But, even joking about the aging process doesn't alleviate some of the fears and frustrations. Losing strength, not being able to see as well, forgetting things that once were so simple—it's not easy. And many people simply give in to the process. They begin to think and act old.

But not Amelia Zortmann. This seventy-nine-year-old Kansas woman collects used clothing for Feed the Children. I'm not talking about a sack or two of clothing; this feisty woman goes all over the Fowler, Kansas, area gathering enough to fill a semi truck. She collected so much that her children built a large storage barn to house all the contributions she receives.

"Everybody is capable of giving," she says, shrugging off any notion that it's unusual for a woman her age to do what she does. "Some people may not care or they're just too busy with themselves. I don't know. But, there's a place for everybody and something for everybody to do. All you got to do is find that place."

And Amelia keeps finding her place! A while ago, she visited the Rose Bud Indian Reservation where much of the clothing she had collected was sent. While she was there, she heard that a family needed help relocating off the reservation. So, Amelia jumped in with both feet, and you can imagine what happened next! Since then she has moved a second family off the reservation, and she continues to give herself away to people in need.

I like the way the psalmist writes about aging: "Those who have been transplanted into the Lord's household, they shall flourish in the courtyards of our God. In old age they shall still be bearing fruit. They shall be full of life and vitality" (Psalm 92:13, 14 MLB).

Life allows no substitutions, no time to go back and replace sunrises and sunsets with another. Each day is new. Embrace the moment. Longfellow said it more eloquently:

> Trust no future, howe'er pleasant
> Let the dead Past bury its dead!
> Act, act in the living Present!
> Heart within and God o'erhead.

LESSONS FROM THE TREES

Tree diary

If you have a large tree on your property, that tree has a very interesting story to tell. It can reveal some startling facts such as when there were other trees in the vicinity, what years there were unusual summer seasons, and when it was attacked by disease. All of this is kept in the diary of the tree—its tree rings.

In the same way as the tree rings record the history of a tree, so our lives are a diary of our past—both the good times and the bad. Our diary records the interesting and the startling, as well as the rough and tough times. One of the rich rewards of growing older is recalling the many rich memories we have—the good times that we enjoyed and the bad ones that we survived.

In 1 Samuel 7:12, Samuel realized how important it was to remember how God had blessed him, so he built a memorial and called it Ebenezer, which means, "hitherto hath the Lord helped us." It was a solid symbol of the Lord's presence up to that point.

The tree has its diary of past victories and defeats; the diary of our lives reveals how God has led us. And knowing that, we can have the assurance of His presence in the future as well. Our diary—our life—tells it all.

9

Despair:

Finding hope for tomorrow

This mad sea shows his teeth tonight,
He curls his lips, he lies in wait,
With lifted teeth, as if to bite!
Brave Admiral, say but one good word:
What shall we do when hope is gone?

"Sail on! Sail on! Sail on! And on!"

JOAQUIN MILLER

I'll never forget Saulala, Honduras. It's a desolate and dreary place. Malaria and respiratory diseases are rampant. It rains almost ten months out of the year. It is one of the wettest and most humid climates I have ever visited.

Just five miles from the Nicaraguan border, Saulala is one of forty villages along the banks of the Coco River that the Honduran government has designated for refugees. More than 250 people settled here in 1981 when Pastor Candido Taylor fled with most of his church congregation from bordering Nicaragua. They brought few possessions, except for the things they were able to carry with them when they fled for their lives.

These people are Miskito Indians, who historically

have had very little interest in governments outside their own villages. That was so until the Sandinistas of Nicaragua decided to create a zone for national security along the Coco River and began burning and destroying the villages of the peaceful Miskitos. The troops tortured and killed as they cleared out the area. One man tearfully told me that the soldiers killed five of his relatives and threw their bodies in a well. Then, they forced the two surviving family members into the well on top of the bodies and buried them alive. Other people in the village had similar stories of horror. If any group of people has ever had a right to despair, it is these people.

So, when they asked me to meet with them in their grass-thatched church, I wondered what words of comfort I could bring. The powdered milk and clothing we had brought in had said in a very tangible way that we cared about them and their struggle, but they needed words of hope for the future.

As one interpreter translated my words into Spanish and a second interpreter from Spanish into Miskito, I told them, "I know you want to go home. That's why I'm going to join you in prayer to believe God that He's going to open the way for you to go back home.

"I want you to know that God said to the children of Israel, 'I have seen your sorrow and seen your affliction. . . .' And as surely as God led His children of old to the Promised Land, He will sustain you until you're able to return home."

Yet, even as I spoke, the faces of the older people told me they wondered if they would die in this strange land, cut off from familiar places and friends, and be buried in this dreary land of despair. And nothing I said could alleviate the threat of such a fate. The despair they felt was evident.

You may feel like you're experiencing the same kind of despair—the feeling that life will never be the same, the feeling that nothing can be done to take away the darkness that clouds your soul. You may be about to break under the weight of your bitterness.

The people at Saulala are discovering that no matter which side of the river they live on, they have to find ways to rise above their circumstances. There were problems on the other side of the river, too. Life is not living without problems; it's facing the problems we have. Their situation is hopeless only if they let it be hopeless—and these courageous people are not going to be defeated. They're living on the wrong side of the river, but they *do* have a place to wait. They see no light at the end of the tunnel, but while they fumble in the darkness, they *can* support and encourage one another.

Once a month, they do something which symbolizes their attitude of hope in the midst of seeming despair. Led by Pastor Taylor, they march up the path toward a hill that allows them to look across the river into their homeland of Nicaragua. With memories of home flooding their hearts, they sing songs of praise.

I can't remember when I've witnessed a more touching scene. Accompanied by the strings of an old guitar, slightly out of tune, they joined together and sang "What a Friend We Have in Jesus." Although they sang in Miskito, I knew the familiar words of the hymn, and the tears flowed down my face as I watched and listened.

> *Have we trials and temptations?*
> *Is there trouble anywhere?*
> *We should never be discouraged,*
> *Take it to the Lord in prayer.*

Can we find a friend so faithful,
Who will all our sorrows share?
Jesus knows our every weakness,
Take it to the Lord in prayer.

What inspiring words of comfort! It was a tremendous experience to see that, after five years of exile, these homeless people could still sing songs of faith.

I believe there are ways you, too, can rise above the mire of despair which threatens to trap and break you.

1. Wait on the Lord.

Not being able to "see the light at the end of the tunnel" causes most of us to become fearful and depressed when a despairing situation comes our way. But, "delay does not always mean denial," someone has wisely said. It may be in situations such as these that we simply have to wait—yes, even when that waiting makes us feel we have been forgotten or neglected.

Many times bitter experiences put us on hold, and for twentieth-century Americans, that's not easy to handle. We live life in the fast lane, eat fast food, and watch movies that condense a person's entire life into a one-hour script. TV commercials depict problems and solve them in thirty seconds or less. We are accustomed to instant gratification. Still, there are times when we simply have to wait on the Lord, as painful as that may be.

But God promises to be with us during the wait. In Psalm 62:5, David writes, "Wait . . . upon God; for my expectation is from him." Then, three verses later, he encourages us to trust in the Lord at "all times," not "most times," but *all* times, because all the power of heaven and earth belongs to the Lord (verse 11, *see also* Matthew 28:18). We can trust in the good times, in impossible times, when things are going well and when they're not.

The Miskito Indians along the Coco River understand this. The Sandinistas have made decisions which have left the Miskitos homeless, but they cannot dictate how these Christian believers should react to the situation. The Miskito Indians haven't slammed the door in God's face by giving up and determining that their plight is hopeless. They're leaving the door open so that God can intervene.

It takes a lot of patience to wait on the Lord, especially for people like the Miskito Indians. But I believe we have to look at our situation in that light. It may not be the best we're hoping for; our dream may be on hold. But, while we're "waiting for the bus to arrive," so to speak, our lives are still going on, and we have to strive for as much quality as possible during those enforced times of waiting.

A few years ago, I took a plane to Milwaukee via Chicago's O'Hare Field. As can happen when flying, Chicago's airport was socked in with fog. Our captain told us that they expected the fog to lift, but until it did, we would be circling the airport. It was an unexpected, enforced time of waiting. I had so many things to do that I had brought along with me that it didn't bother me; I just kept right on working. But the man in the seat next to me really began to fume, as did others. They were worried about their connections, they were frustrated at having to fly around and around in a circle; in short, they were not using this time to any good advantage. Down times and unexpected waiting periods must be accepted as necessary holding periods. In the same way that no one on our flight would have wanted the pilot to risk our lives by trying to land, so we have to accept the enforced wait as being in our best interests—to wait for the fog to lift.

One of our Feed the Children telephone volunteers is a

widow who had a difficult time adjusting to her husband's death. She was depressed and discouraged and believed she would never again find anything to live for. Out of desperation, she volunteered to answer telephones, more to fill up her time than out of a desire to contribute. "You know what happened, Larry?" she said to me one evening. "As I listened to the heartaches of people who called in, as I counseled with them, I helped myself." She learned an important lesson. Life may be on hold; it may not look good. But, when you go on living, the despair goes away much faster.

Wait on the Lord, but don't give up on life while you wait.

2. Keep on keeping on.

There's a story about the poet Joaquin Miller, who spent a lot of time reading the ship's log that Columbus kept during his 1492 voyage. As he sailed the waters of the uncharted Atlantic, Columbus wrote the same words day after day, "This day we sailed on." Miller became intrigued and inspired as he read those words each day, entry after entry.

Storms had ravaged the ships; the *Pinta* had lost her rudder; the men were threatening mutiny. Conditions couldn't have been worse. Columbus must have been on the verge of despair. Yet, he had set his course, and nothing could turn him from it. Through danger, darkness, hunger, panic, and exhaustion, they *sailed on*.

From the inspiration of that moment, Miller sat down and penned the words to the poem "Columbus." In one section of the poem, the mate is discouraged and turns to Columbus:

> *This mad sea shows his teeth tonight,*
> *He curls his lips, he lies in wait,*
> *With lifted teeth, as if to bite!*
> *Brave Admiral, say but one good word:*
> *What shall we do when hope is gone?*

> *"Sail on! Sail on! Sail on! And on!"*

What a magnificent epic of perseverance! What courage it took to sail on in the midst of such uncertainty. But, as you know, Columbus's despair did not last forever. The shores of a new world became his to conquer.

Sometimes when everything around you seems hopeless, the only thing you can do is *sail on*. When you don't know what faces you in the darkness of your despair, you *sail on* anyway in faith that whatever comes your way, God will give you the strength and courage to reach your destination.

3. Get outside yourself.

When I was still pastoring, there was a lady who was so despairing about her situation. No matter what anyone did, it was not enough. Her problems loomed so large that no solution was adequate. As a consequence, she kept drawing into her own little world, alienating friends, and cutting off any possible help she might find.

Finally, one day I drove over to her house and told her to get in the car and go with me on a trip. I had used part of our church's mission money to buy groceries for a family whose children were malnourished and almost starving. I had this lady carry in the groceries and give them to the mother, and then visit with the kids and see their pure joy at the sight of food. Without my saying a word, it made an impact on her that she never forgot. Her world was not nearly as bad as she had thought. But she needed to get out of herself before she could realize it.

In 2 Corinthians 1:4, Paul explains that God comforts us in our tribulation, "that we may be able to comfort them which are in any trouble, by the comfort wherewith we ourselves are comforted of God." That's also the definition of evangelism: "One beggar sharing with another beggar where to find Bread." Therein lies one of the keys to conquering despair, namely, getting outside yourself and talking to others of your victories and how you've been helped. If you're alone in your despair, you have a tendency to look inward. But if you're sharing with others, you're sharing your victories, not your losses.

There's an old Swedish saying, "Blessed is he who sees a dawn in every midnight." When we share with others, we are enabled to envision the sun that's shining in the midst of the darkness.

4. Know that God is in command.

God hasn't abandoned the world, and He hasn't abandoned you. From His vantage point as the sovereign Lord of history, He still controls the affairs of men and women and looks after those who belong to Him through Christ.

I remember trying to make a particularly tough decision, spending hours wrestling with my dilemma. Finally, I made a decision, although I was not fully convinced I had made the right one. That day during my prayer time, I opened the Bible and read, "The Lord reigns; let the earth rejoice" (Psalm 97:1 RSV). As I read the verse, I felt a sense of peace and contentment. It dawned on me that it didn't matter what decision I made, because all power belongs to the Lord, and He would be with me, regardless of my choice.

In his poem "The Hollow Men," T. S. Eliot pessimistically says, "This is the way the world ends, not with a bang, but with a whimper." And in moments of despair, you may feel that your life will end, and no one will know the difference. Your despair may convince you that no one cares what happens to you or what you do. But, don't you believe it! You can face every day with confidence and courage knowing that you belong to a God who loves and cares for you.

Every time I think of despair, I think of Daniel in the lions' den. Can't you just imagine him sitting there among those animals? One crunch of their mouths, one swipe of their paws, and he would be finished. What a horrible and painful way to die! Surely, Daniel wondered if the God he served would deliver him; surely, he wondered if anyone really cared what happened to him. Daniel served a Lord God who cared. You remember the story—the king arrived at the den, after keeping Daniel there overnight, and cried fearfully, "Daniel, O Daniel, servant of the living God, is thy God, whom thou servest continually, able to deliver thee from the lions?"

And Daniel's reply was heard throughout the kingdom. "O king, live forever. My God hath sent his angel, and hath shut the lions' mouths." Daniel was taken up out of the den, and "no manner of hurt was found upon him, because he believed in his God." What a picture of calmness in the midst of chaos! (See Daniel 6.)

You, too, can have that assurance when the "lions of despair" threaten your faith and threaten to break your spirit. The same God who delivered Daniel from the den of lions will calm and comfort you in your darkest moments.

James Russell Lowell knew this when he wrote these lines in his poem "The Present Crisis":

Truth forever on the scaffold,
Wrong forever on the throne;
Yet that scaffold sways the future
And behind the dim unknown
Standeth God within the shadow,
Keeping watch above his own.

If you believe that, nothing the world can throw at you will break you. God is standing in the shadow keeping watch over His own. Despair will not overtake you, and bitterness will not be able to eat away at your soul.

LESSONS FROM THE TREES

The bark beetle

Ninety percent of the trees destroyed by insects are killed by the tiny bark beetle. It bores into the inner bark and lays eggs in the criss-crossed tunnels. When the eggs hatch, the larvae feed on the bark, and sooner or later the tree dies. It's difficult to believe that something as small as a bark beetle can kill a giant tree. But, each year thousands of trees are killed because of this tiny insect.

Despair and hopelessness can creep into our lives just like the bark beetle, and almost before we know it. Allowed to grow, they soon consume and destroy our strength, threatening the essence of our being. Like "the little foxes, that spoil the vine, " it's the little beetles that kill the tree.

If you've allowed despair to take over your life, call on the God who is bigger than your despair. He's the one who knows both the pain of the past and present, but also the possibilities of your future. Together, you can wipe out the threat to your future and become the healthy, happy person you want to be and that God intends you to be.

PART

Attitude Adjustments:

Improving the conditions that hinder healthy growth

10

Guilt:

How to find peace

"If we confess our sins, he is faithful and just to forgive us our sins, and to cleanse us from all unrighteousness."

1 John 1:9

I knew the young woman was troubled the minute she walked up to me. Her eyes darted back and forth, and her lips quivered when she asked if I would talk with her for a few minutes. I had just finished speaking about the three giants young people face (drugs, sex, and alcohol) in her high school assembly, and it was obvious my talk had opened up a painful wound. We found a private place, and she began crying as she told her story.

A few months back, she had gotten pregnant. Because she wasn't married, her pregnancy was a source of embarrassment to her family, and her mother insisted that she get an abortion to "save the family name." Although the girl did not want the abortion, she agreed to it, succumbing to the pressures her anxious mother applied. The abortion solved the mother's embarrassment, but it created another problem, one not so easily dismissed. "My mother got rid of the baby," the girl said bitterly, "but she can't get rid of my guilt." And the weight of her burden was pushing her to the point of breaking.

Guilt is a powerful negative force which, if left unchecked and unresolved, can become as deadly as a cancer inside our bodies. Some people bear the weight of guilt in resigned silence, not wanting to believe that anything or anyone can absolve them from the feelings they carry. Others make excuses for their actions, not really accepting responsibility for what has happened. They play what I call the "blame game," transferring blame for their own guilt to someone else or to circumstances beyond their control. They spend their time making up excuses instead of confessing their guilt. Either way it's handled, guilt is not resolved and it continues to grow and fester.

That's why I believe that of all human emotions, guilt is one of the most destructive, because guilt feelings occur when we do something we know we should not have done. We can remember what we did; we know when it happened; we can see the results; and it seems next to impossible to quit blaming ourselves for having done it. Many of us walk around, day after day, carrying the same load of guilt, not knowing how to rid ourselves of its burden.

Karl Menninger, the well-known psychiatrist, in his book *Whatever Became of Sin*, tells about walking along the streets of New York City with a friend when they encountered a man who was hollering, "You're guilty! You're guilty!" Pedestrians crossed to the other side of the street to avoid him or carefully turned the other way. As Menninger and his friend walked past the shouting man, Menninger turned to his friend and said, "How did he know?" Of course, Menninger's point was that we all feel guilty about something. How we handle that guilt determines whether or not we break under the weight of bitterness and self-recrimination.

In the book *A Gift of Hope*, Robert Veninga writes, "Sometimes other people need to give us permission to rid ourselves of guilt. But most of the time we need to forgive ourselves. How do you diminish guilt? Unfortunately, there is no easy formula, no sure guarantee. Guilt is one of the strongest and most difficult emotions to conquer."

We have to understand the finality of the forgiveness of Christ. Christ died that we might live. His sacrifice atones for our sin. He offers the way for us to cleanse our souls of sin and guilt.

Several years ago, a prominent retired U.S. senator called a press conference. He was terminally ill and realized he had little time to live. Wracked with guilt, he told the news media gathered around him, "One of the last things I did as a senator was to testify before a special investigative committee. Today, it's important for me to tell you that some of my testimony was not true. I lied. I ask your forgiveness."

Many people, like that senator, wait until they're dying or at the point of breaking before they do something about the guilt they suffer. But what a price to pay! What a waste of human energy!

According to Webster's Dictionary, guilt is a feeling of culpability caused by a breach of conduct. Anyone who has suffered from the sharp and insistent pangs of guilt knows what that means. Even small children who do something they've been told not to do understand the feelings associated with guilt. Caught in the act, they come with pleading eyes, wanting someone to hug them and reassure them that even though they've done something they shouldn't, they're still loved. The need to have that kind of forgiveness never leaves us, no matter how old we become.

When I was in high school, I stepped next door from my parents' barber shop to the "ten-cent store" and stole a forty-nine-cent fountain pen. What possessed me to do that I'll never know, but I did. Later, I went to college and then on to theology school. Yet every time I came back home and went to Dad's barber shop, I thought about the fountain pen. Here I was in school, studying to be a minister, and I was carrying around the guilt of that act. Finally, one day, I went into the store and paid the store a dollar for the pen I had stolen so long ago. I could have saved myself a lot of agony had I done that simple act of confession much earlier, but I didn't. And somehow, the act became more reprehensible the longer I carried its weight within me.

Several years ago, I was preaching in another city when a middle-aged man named Bob hung around after the service waiting to talk with me. As I was leaving, he said, "Larry, could I talk to you privately?"

Naturally, I said he could, so we went over to my car and within seconds he began to spill out a painful story of wrongdoing. Talk about guilt—he was loaded down with it! I listened and tried to understand, and I asked him, "Have you prayed about it? Have you asked God to forgive you for it?"

He said, "Larry, there have been nights I've never gotten in bed, but stayed on my knees crying and begging God for forgiveness. But I still have that gnawing feeling inside. And every time I see the people I wronged I have a sharp pain. They don't even know that I'm the one who did it."

I said to him, "Bob, I'm going to pray with you and I want to lead you in the sinner's prayer. God will forgive you. I know that. The Bible promises it, Jesus died that it might happen, and I've personally experienced it in my own life."

And we did just that. I can still hear him crying; I don't think I've heard a grown man cry any harder. It seemed like pain just gushed out. Finally, it subsided. After a while, we talked some more and he said, "Larry, it feels like a great weight has been lifted."

I knew what he meant, but I was still puzzled. I said, "Bob, I've seen you in prayer at church. You said you have prayed all night sometimes. What was different this time?"

What he said gave me an insight I'd never before realized: "Larry, there's not another person in the world that knows I've done what I told you about. I had to tell another person as well as God."

That caught me off guard, but I kept thinking about it. To my surprise, the following afternoon, one of the pastors in the community we were in said, "Larry, I just heard about ——" and he told me about Bob.

I was flabbergasted. Just twelve hours previously I was the only person who knew what had happened. Now everyone did. I discovered that Bob had gone to every person he had wronged, had confessed what he had done, and told them about meeting with me. Then he described what he was going to do to make things right. Later, I went to visit him and he was like a new man. There was a smile on his face, an honesty in his conversation, and a confidence that things were going to work out.

I hope it did; it was not going to be easy, because he had committed some serious offenses. But I've never forgotten the lessons I learned there. That man experienced a reality that we Christians sometimes forget. We don't live in church; we don't spend twenty-four hours a day in prayer; we are not a soul only. Rather, we are creatures of

God living in the world with other creatures. That's why it's necessary many times not only to make peace with God, but also to make peace with our fellow human beings. In other words, the first step to forgiveness is the *vertical* dimension of our life; God is the sin forgiver. But, we must also address the *horizontal* dimension of life as well. Here's what I mean:

1. Confess your guilt to God.

The most important place to begin anything is with God. To be at peace with our heavenly Father is our most important task. That's why we must first confess our guilt to Him.

In the parable of the prodigal son, Jesus made it clear that forgiveness did not have to be earned. When the prodigal son came home, he was not asked to account for his spending; he was not asked to defend his sinful actions. He was simply received back into the household with open arms. And, most importantly, the son accepted this unconditional love. He did not say, "I don't deserve it." In thanksgiving, he received his father's love. (*See* Luke 15:11–24.)

One of the greatest barriers to resolving guilt is the unwillingness to believe that forgiveness can be ours. Many people live with guilt because they think it's fair punishment for their sin or for having done something of which they are ashamed.

But, the load of guilt you carry can be lifted from you—not just lightened, but taken away. That's the essence of the Gospel of Jesus Christ. And it is available to all who seek it. I like the way the *Living Bible* paraphrases the powerful verse in Hebrews that promises us forgiveness: "I will never again remember their sins and lawless deeds" (Hebrews 10:17 TLB). What a promise! *Never again!*

The wonderful thing about God's forgiveness is the "forgetfulness" that goes along with it. I might not be able to forget the act. You may not be able to forget that it was done. But God says He not only forgives, but He forgets. His forgiveness is 100 percent!

That forgiveness was all made possible through the Cross. When Jesus uttered His last words, "It is finished," He sacrificed His life for the redemption of our sins. He paid the ultimate price; He paid with His life. And the finality of that act allows us to say with confidence and faith that forgiveness can be ours. Nothing anyone can say or do can take it away or diminish its power.

This unconditional love leaves us open and free to start over. Pythagoras taught his disciples the familiar saying, "Leave not the mark of the pot upon the ashes." In other words, wipe out the past, forget it, and start the day fresh. 1 John 1:9 states, "If we confess our sins, he is faithful and just to forgive us our sins, and to cleanse us from all unrighteousness."

The great evangelist Billy Graham once remarked that he had been criticized for almost everything he did, at one time or another. But, there was one thing he could never remember anyone faulting him for. "I have never been criticized for inviting people to come forward and ask forgiveness of their sins," Dr. Graham said. "Even my worst detractors understand the need for forgiveness."

2. Confess your guilt to someone significant in your life.

Although I didn't realize it at the time, I was a significant person to Bob. He needed someone he respected to hear what he had done. The only way that God could reach him was through someone else.

Dr. O. Hobart Mower, a clinical psychologist, suggests that one of the ways we rid ourselves of guilt is by confessing the cause of the guilt to the one we've wronged or to someone we consider to be significant. It's important to note that sometimes we can't confess to the one we've wronged because it might cause even more hurt and damage. That's why telling another significant person may be appropriate.

But here's a word of caution: choose carefully the person you confess to. Make sure it is someone who will hold your confession in confidence. Choose someone who is strong, who is capable of hearing the confession and maybe even forgetting it after you tell your story. Choose someone who has struggled with the same problem or who has the ability to understand your struggle. Otherwise, telling a weaker person may only compound your problem.

Although confession is a risk, it's an important part of the healing process. Jesus affirmed our need to confess to one another in James 5:16 RSV: "Therefore confess your sins to one another, and pray for one another, that you may be healed."

It's amazing what one simple act of confession can do. I remember when, as a child, I threw rocks at a group of children who lived at the end of our street. As luck would have it, one of the children ran to my mother and told on me. Well, my mother was not one to let things go by unnoticed! She spanked me soundly, and then said, "Go tell those children that you're sorry you threw rocks at them." That was about the last thing on earth I wanted to do, but I also knew when my mother said to do something, I'd better do it.

With fear and trembling, I slowly walked to the end of the street and mumbled my apology. But, you know, as I headed back up the street to my house, I felt much better.

I was no longer the neighborhood "bad guy." My friends liked me again, and my mother was pleased. The guilt that I had felt a few minutes earlier had been removed. That lesson has stayed with me—in my marriage, in my relationships at work, and in my dealings with friends and business associates.

When guilt and fear keep you paralyzed, it's important to confess the cause of your guilt to God; many times, it may be necessary also to confess that guilt to a significant person. That may be a minister, a best friend, even a counselor. Whomever you choose, your confession to a significant person may be the way God chooses to bring inner peace to you.

3. Forgive the person who has wronged you.

Forgiving someone who has caused you pain is a very difficult thing to do. It's much easier to talk about than it is to erase the feelings of anger and hurt. I remember talking to a woman whose father had left the family for another woman when she was ten years old. It was not so much the leaving that was painful as it was the way in which he left.

"I don't want anything more to do with the kids," he told his wife. As his eight children listened, he said, "If you can't take care of them yourself, call the welfare department." And with that, he left and never returned.

Years later, the woman harbored a hatred for her father that had festered and grown out of proportion, and the scars of rejection made it difficult for her to live her life to the fullest. Worst of all, she felt guilty for hating her father so much.

"Why don't you write your father a letter," I suggested, "and tell him that you forgive him?"

Almost before the words were out of my mouth, she blurted out, "But, I don't know where he is."

"Write the letter anyway," I persisted, "and then do two things: First, whenever you think about your father and all he did to you, go get the letter and read it. Read your words of forgiveness, and then redirect your feelings. Second, if you ever find your father, give him the letter. But, even if you don't find him, keep the letter in your heart and mind as if he had read it and had accepted your forgiveness."

Even if you have every reason in the world to be angry and hurt, you cannot afford to carry around those kinds of feelings. Forgive and forget. It's an old cliché, but it works.

4. Make right the wrong you've done or the wrong someone else has done to you.

Because guilt is caused by an act or acts that create a breach, it is important to heal this gap. Time heals some of the wound, but action can speed up the process. Through Jesus Christ we are able not only to correct our mistakes but to be continually renewed in Him.

A school teacher once told me a story about a young girl who was a student in her French class. Every morning, the girl came in before school just to chat with the teacher, and over the months they developed a special bond of friendship. But one day, the teacher saw the student copying test answers from her neighbor's paper. When the teacher confronted her, she immediately confessed and asked the teacher to forgive her.

"Even though I accepted her apology and forgave her," the teacher said, "I realized in a few days that our special relationship had changed. A barrier had been erected between us that would not go away.

"I knew this student would never feel comfortable with me again unless she did something to restore herself in my good graces. So, the next day I asked her to help me grade papers and then suggested that each morning for the next two weeks she come in and work for me."

Not surprisingly, she faithfully appeared each day, and by the end of two weeks, the friendship was back to normal. By her extra hours of work, she had been enabled to "right the wrong" she'd done.

In our society, criminals are forced to "pay for their crimes" by serving time in our penal institutions, and, in some cases, by giving up their lives. A criminal once told Leslie D. Weatherhead that although he had not been caught and was intellectually certain he could never have been discovered, the burden of guilt for the crime he committed had been so intolerable that he had walked into Scotland Yard and given himself up. Even though he suffered drastic and inescapable punishment externally, the peace he felt internally was worth it, he said.

And so it may be for you. Try these simple steps. Work at it until the load is lifted and the burden is gone. Do what it takes to bring health and healing to your soul. And know that God through Christ is present with you each step of the way.

There's a story about Saint Augustine that illustrates how we need to pray for forgiveness for our sins:

> At first, when his life seemed empty and unfulfilled, he prayed, "O God, forgive me of all my sins—but not yet."
>
> But when the emptiness of his life began to engulf him, he cried out, "O God, forgive me for all my sins—save one."
>
> Finally, though, he realized that peace could only come when he prayed, "O God, forgive me for all my sins—and do it now. Amen!"

LESSONS FROM THE TREES

Pruning

Pruning means shortening branches and twigs, and cutting out old, worn stems and weak shoots. By thinning and pruning the places where there are too many small branches and twigs, the growth of the tree is aided. Pruning allows light and air to flow more freely throughout the branches. As a result, the tree is healthier, stronger, and less subject to disease. In transplanted trees, pruning also compensates for the roots lost in moving, and thereby helps the tree maintain a more natural balance between its top and bottom.

Many times, like the tree, our lives get out of balance. Emotions like guilt and shame can crowd out our positive feelings until we feel as though we're going to break under their weight. Left alone, these feelings can corrode our mind, soul, and body. That's when a pruning lesson becomes important. Guilt must be addressed; shame must be faced; a pruning must be effected. And although pruning creates temporary wounds, it allows new and more positive growth eventually to occur. If you need pruning in your life, accept it as God's wonderful method of giving you healing.

11

Doubt:

How to make your faith stronger

"The line is, if you are broken, don't despair. Bounce back as soon as you can."

JEREMIAH DENTON
Prisoner of war in North Vietnam

Of all the problems and bitter experiences that one can have, none is more destructive than a loss of faith. When faith is gone and doubt overtakes, nothing is left but the bitterness of the reality of the moment. No Lord to lean on; no Christ to turn to; no answer for yesterday, today, and forever.

"When faith is lost, when honor dies, the man is dead!" the poet John Greenleaf Whittier wrote. So when someone tells me that they've lost their faith . . . that their doubts have conquered them . . . that they no longer believe . . . I take it seriously, because loss of faith is one of the most serious problems any of us could ever face.

I have seen mothers whose babies were starving, and the only thing they had left was their faith. I've seen fathers lose their jobs, their homes, even their families, but the one thing they had left was their faith. Keeping our faith alive and well is our number-one task as human beings. No matter how bitter the experience, how devastating the loss, how impoverishing the reality, one can still have faith. We still have God to lean upon. There is a Way of Escape.

Yet having said that, I have to say something that seems to contradict it: there is nothing harder than keeping your faith alive and well when the injustices and cruelties of life leave you defeated and wondering why God has permitted such bitter things to happen. There is nothing harder than looking for comfort when there are no answers.

During the worst part of Ethiopia's drought, when hundreds of thousands were dying from starvation, I watched ninety-one people die in one day at a camp named Bati. As body after body was taken to the makeshift tent that was used for a morgue, I began to ask, "Why? Why, God, is this happening?" My faith was shaken in a way that it had never been tested before.

I remember comforting a mother whose baby had just died. She cried, "Weiya, weiya, weiya!" which sounded like "Why? Why? Why?" in English. One of our co-workers explained that to the Ethiopians who knew her tragedy, she was saying, "My daughter is dead; how can I go on living?" Although I didn't understand the language, I, too, knew what she was saying and I wept with her, wondering as she was, where the justice of it was.

It's easy to have faith when everything is going well, but when problems arise, we begin doubting God. Biblical scholar Alan Redpath didn't really understand doubt until he was about sixty-five years old. At that time, he suffered a stroke and, for a time, was reduced to almost childhood. In his helpless condition, he sank to the depths of despair. Instead of finding comfort and solace in the faith which he had studied and written about for most of his life, he began to doubt God's love for him and the promises that had brought him comfort in the past. And, of course, for a man whose whole life had been dedicated to spreading the Gospel, he felt angry and confused.

Only then did he really begin to experience the kind of faith he had preached for years. Only when he himself was experiencing the bitterness of life did he begin to find the antidote which faith has. The result was that he became a new man, a new preacher, and a new practitioner of the Gospel.

"It is cynicism and fear that freeze life," Harry Emerson Fosdick wrote. "It is faith that thaws it out, releases it, sets it free." But what do you do when you lose your faith, when doubt takes over, when your confidence in Christ is gone?

The Apostle Thomas once appeared before the risen Christ concerned to find proof that Christ had indeed risen from the dead. Jesus showed His nail-scarred hands and the wound in His side from the sword. Thomas at once confessed his faith and Jesus blessed him. Then He added this comment, "Blessed are they that have not seen, and yet have believed" (John 20:29). In other words, it was great that Thomas had believed upon seeing proof; it was even more blessed to have believed without proof.

That's not easy to do. All around us people live their lives as if there were no God, no Christ, and no tomorrow. It's not easy to go against the grain. It's not easy to profess faith when others are not. Here are the things I recommend to restore faith and to conquer doubt:

1. Be honest before God.

Prayer is the one place where we cannot lie. That is one of the reasons I've always believed that it is essential to pray daily. People can lie to friends, family, and acquaintances, but it's futile to lie to God. God knows our hearts and minds, and God seeks an honest heart above all else. So, when doubt seeks to take the victory out of your life, go to God in prayer and honesty. Confess your doubts, your loss of faith. Tell Him the whys and the hows. Don't leave anything out.

That will do two things for you. First, when you confess your doubts out loud, they cease to be a skeleton in the closet. God knows your problems and you've confessed them to Him. You won't have to fear being haunted by them any longer. Second, there is something about saying them aloud that takes some of the edge off of them. You will realize that they aren't as big or bad as you thought. So, open up and be honest before God. Doubt cannot shatter faith because faith says, "My heart trusts even though my mind doubts."

2. Live it even when you doubt it.

When you're having problems of faith, it's almost impossible to work through them intellectually. You can read every book in the world or talk to some of the smartest persons in the world, and still have your problem. But the real problems of faith are resolved in the arena of life. Oswald Chambers once said, "God does not give us overcoming life. He gives us life as we overcome." Doubt becomes faith in the struggle of existence, not in the world of intellect.

In Mark 4, Jesus relates the parable of the sower. In verses sixteen and seventeen, He compares those who give up easily to those seeds that are sown on stony ground. In the midst of the vicissitudes of life, they perish quickly. Their roots are inadequate. And in life, doubt can overcome the seed of faith.

Nothing is a better example of faith than the colored pictures in a spring seed catalog. Isn't it incredible that little tiny seeds can be put into dirt and in a matter of weeks be beautiful flowers? The same is true with your life. Your faith seems so small now; you feel there's no way that you can turn your doubt around. But when you start living faith, even if you're having trouble believing it, something miraculous occurs: you began to see God's hand at work in all parts of your life. As you strive to practice faith, you see faithful acts occurring. You find the proofs for faith in the living.

3. Know that all of life has a measure of uncertainty.

The person who never has any questions or doubts isn't alive. We cannot prove another person's love; we cannot prove that we will be healthy tomorrow; nor can we prove that we will have a job tomorrow. Life is always lived with more or with less uncertainty. That is as true for faith as it is the rest of life.

This does not mean we shouldn't do all we can to be full of faith. "The only limit to our realization of tomorrow will be our doubts of today," Franklin D. Roosevelt said. We can't cease to take care of our bodies physically any less than we can refuse to be concerned about our souls. We can't take chances with danger either on the highways of our nation or the highway of our soul. We have to work at our jobs to survive financially and work at the job of keeping our faith alive and vibrant—even when we have doubts.

When the disciples were on the Sea of Galilee and a sudden storm arose, they were terrified. Finally, they had enough presence of mind to take their eyes off the storm and put them on Jesus, who slept in the bottom of the boat.

We, too, at times in our lives must take our eyes off the uncertainty of the moment and focus on Jesus Christ. We must make the big shift from the problem to the solution.

4. Doubt your doubts.

I have a minister friend whose adult son was struggling with his doubts. The young man was also considering the ministry but, because of some unanswered questions, he was having second thoughts. His father very wisely listened to him and encouraged his son to talk. After one such session, my friend said, "Son, I can't resolve your doubts for you. You're a man now, and it's up to you to resolve them yourself. I'll talk with you, I'll pray for you, and I'll be hoping for you to make the right choices. But, there's one suggestion that I want you to consider. After you've wrestled with your doubts about the answers of faith, spend some time doubting the doubts."

Doubt your doubts! Be certain about the uncertain. We have to trust God with the unexplainable. Know that faith says our hearts can trust even when our mind doubts.

When you feel doubt and fear bending you, like the willow tree, close to the ground, turn to the God that Abraham believed in. "In hope he believed against hope, that he should become the father of many nations; as he had been told. . . . He did not weaken in faith when he considered his own body, which was as good as dead because he was about a hundred years old. . . . No distrust made him waver concerning the promise of God, but he grew strong in his faith as he gave glory to God, fully convinced that God was able to do what he had promised" (Romans 4:18–21 RSV).

In America, we like to live life in the fast lane, eat fast foods, and drive fast cars. Like the tape recorders that are so much a part of our lives, we often live life on *fast forward*. But any time we have difficulty or doubt, it seems like we've been put on *pause*. We may not like it, and we may fight against it, but that's the time we need to stop and listen to God. As the psalmist put it, "Be still and know that I am God" (Psalm 46:10). He is God when we believe and when we don't; He is God when we struggle and when we fall. It's impossible not to doubt sometimes, but doubt your doubts also.

5. Feed your doubts the Word of God.

I know that kind of advice sounds unorthodox, but it came from a great evangelist of the nineteenth century, Dwight L. Moody. He related that he was struggling with doubt when he thought to himself, *My, wouldn't it be great if I could just go to the store and buy a bucket of faith to help me overcome my doubts.* Later, he was reading in the Bible and came across Romans 10:17 which reads, "So then faith cometh by hearing, and hearing by the word of God." He said it was almost an instant revelation: *the Bible is food for the soul.* The Bible addresses our doubts and stirs our faith.

One of my favorite stories about reading the Bible is about a young boy whose mother was concerned that he was so quiet. She went to the door of his room and said, "What are you doing?"

He answered, "I'm watching Jesus raise Lazarus from the dead."

She opened the door and saw that what he was doing was reading that story in the Bible from John 11. In his mind, he was visualizing how it took place. He was doing it so strongly and vividly that he felt he was actually watching it!

As I've read the great stories of the Bible through the years—Moses at the Red Sea, David facing Goliath, Daniel in the lions' den—it's been helpful to me to visualize how each of those scenes happened. In the process, my faith has been strengthened for the challenges I face.

When you are in a doubting period and struggling to believe, feed your doubts the Word of God, and as you do, try to recreate the events in your mind. Picture the Apostle Paul as he sat in his jail cell saying, "I can do all things through Christ which strengtheneth me (Philippians 4:13). Paint in your mind the picture of Jesus as He carried His cross up Golgatha's hill. Let your soul feed on the inspiration of Scripture. Daily attendance upon the reading of the Bible will do miracles for your faith.

6. God will be present for us even after our doubts.

No matter what you are going through, know that God is not only present in the midst of your struggling faith, but He will also be there when it's over. He still loves and cares for you no matter what. When Peter writes, "Cast all your cares on him for he cares for you" (see 1 Peter 5:7), we sometimes think that only refers to external problems. It also means problems inside as well. Certainly, it includes our doubts. When our faith is gone, doubt overtakes us. That's when we have to take God's Word at its literal best and cast our doubts on Him. With God's help, we can refuse to let one event or any series of events destroy a lifetime of faith.

It will help if you ask yourself the question, "When did I start doubting?" For Alan Redpath, it was in the midst of his illness. For the disciple Thomas, it was after the horror of the Lord's crucifixion. But just as they came through those crisis events, so can you. And when you do, God will be there waiting for you, just as He was before you doubted, while you doubted, and after you passed through your doubts.

When the children of Israel faced some enormous task and it seemed as if God was nowhere to be found, they would pray to the "God of Abraham, Isaac, and Jacob." They knew that of all the Hebrew people, those men had struggled with doubt like no one else had. They, too, had wondered if the sun would ever shine again. They had held fast through their doubts, and one day their faith was rewarded. Just the mere mention of the names of those men was an invitation to stay steady, to know that God was still God, that He had not changed, that He was there for them.

When it looks as if you're going to break, know that God will never leave you. He is there in the midst of your struggle. He is there to help you bend and not break.

One of the most outstanding stories of overcoming doubt that I know of is told by Colonel Robinson Risner in his book *The Passing of the Night.* Colonel Risner spent seven years as a prisoner of war in a North Vietnamese prison camp. Rather than give in to doubt in what seemed like a hopeless situation, Colonel Risner held onto his faith:

> When the pain started really ripping me, I began desperately to pray. I kept quoting a Scripture verse from the Bible over and over: "My grace is sufficient." I thought this meant God would give me grace to bear whatever I had to bear without giving in. But nothing was happening. I cried, "Lord, you promised grace to bear anything. But this pain . . . I can't stand it . . . God! Help me, please help me!"
>
> I don't know how long I endured it—several hours. I was hollering now. Really, it was a scream out of my guts that I couldn't stifle. I was in such pain that it was involuntary. I knew I couldn't last much longer. My will was ebbing away. My guts and determination were shat-

139

tered. I was no longer a man with a mind and body and soul. I had been reduced to a mass of rope and sheer pain. I kept praying. When I saw I wasn't going to be able to hold out any longer, I prayed, "God, you've got to help me. I can't afford to give in. I'd be a traitor." I believed that with all my heart. It was unthinkable that I could be brought to a point where I would have to give in.

Finally I hollered, "Okay, I'll talk." The minute it came out I felt miserable. I had never been so disappointed or had a lower opinion of myself. It was utter contempt. I despised myself for giving in. . . .

Risner was forced to sign a "confession" that he had bombed, strafed, and rocketed the North Vietnamese. Although nothing in his so-called confession hurt the American cause, Risner hated himself for giving in to them. Yet, he never let doubt destroy his faith, even though he had every reason to doubt that he would ever be released from his cell.

As the days turned into years, Risner held onto the belief that he could take his imprisonment for as long as it lasted. And it was this faith, weakened at times by the pain of the moment, that allowed him to hope when there was no hope. When he walked out of the gate of the prison camp after seven long years, he walked out with his faith intact. God had seen him through. God was still the same God before and after prison. The ups and downs of those terrible years had not changed that reality.

Jeremiah Denton, another of our prisoners of war in North Vietnam, has written about the difficulty of knowing when you've violated what you believed in. He said, "The North Vietnamese could break anyone into giving them something, and some of the men were in deep despair because they had been unmercifully tortured into giving biographies and confessions. I passed the word for them to get themselves together. 'The line is, if you are broken, don't despair. Bounce back as soon as you can.' "

That's great advice. *Bounce back.* Don't let your doubts linger long. Don't feed them and nourish them. Bounce back—God will always be there to receive you again.

The cure for doubt is faith that bounces back. One of the great hymns of the church puts it this way:

> *O for a faith that will not shrink*
> *Though pressed by many a foe,*
> *That will not tremble on the brink*
> *Of any earthly woe.*
> *A faith that shines more bright and clear*
> *When tempests rage without,*
> *That, when in danger, knows no fear,*
> *In darkness feels no doubt.*
> *Lord, give me such a faith as this,*
> *And then, whate'er may come,*
> *I'll taste e'en now the hallowed bliss*
> *Of an eternal home.*
>
> WILLIAM BATHURST

The only way out is through faith in Jesus Christ; the way of escape is open to all who believe him.

Galatians 3:22 TLB

LESSONS FROM THE TREES

How cavities start

Trees have cavities just like human beings, but tree cavities originate from neglected bark injuries. Normally, good, sound bark forms a protective barrier for the tender tissues beneath it. But if considerable injury occurs, wood-rotting fungi and boring insects have ample time to enter and cause decay. This prevents healing, and consequently a large cavity is formed.

Doubt often begins like this. We let up on some important dimension of Christian living; then, in time of serious conflict, we're unable to repel the enemy. Doubt attacks the armor of our faith, working to destroy the essence of our hope. If left unattended, we're soon left with nothing but a large void—a cavity—in our soul.

That's why we need to attack doubt when it first begins by searching out the Word of God, seeking God diligently in prayer, and finding support and counsel with fellow Christians. Such efforts will keep our armor strong against the enemy, just like the tree must keep its bark sound and healthy. The result will be a stronger, more overcoming, faith-filled life.

12

Bitter or Better?

Six steps in the right direction

Eskimo definition of *forgiveness*: "Not being able to think about it anymore."

arlier this year, I spent a day with a farmer whose wife had just committed suicide. Totally distraught over their financial circumstances, she had gotten up early, stacked school papers and other combustible material in the yard, and set them on fire. Then, as incredible as it seems, she flung herself into the blazing inferno. The reality that they were going to lose the farm her parents had left her was more than she could take. When her husband awoke, she was dead.

As I listened to him relate this story, I literally hurt inside for him. My mind kept screaming, *This is not fair! Somebody's to blame! How could this have happened in America?* I must confess that there haven't been many times in my life when I felt so totally helpless, without anything to say, but that's the way I felt that day.

I wished that I had been able to visit with his wife beforehand. I wished that I could have gone to the bank with her and talked to the people they owed money to. I wished I could have ministered to her about Christ in her moment of despair. But it was too late for that. All that I could do was be present for her husband as he tried to put his life back together. If there's any lesson to be learned from situations like theirs, it is that life is painful for so many people.

As a minister, I counsel with a lot of people with many different kinds of problems. The problem that they share most often is *disappointment*, feeling that life has treated them unfairly. Their hopes and promises have not been realized. They are frustrated and bitter. And their bitter experiences have led them to be deeply resentful of both life and people.

When I visit with them, I always take them seriously. I know they're telling the truth. And yet, if they want more than someone to listen to them, I also try to help them in other ways. And one of the most effective ways is to help them realize this important point: *everyone's* life is filled with disappointments, disillusionments, and difficulties. Though each situation is different, *everyone* has those times in life when things turn out differently than they wanted or expected. Everyone has those times when they are faced with either bending or breaking.

That's why I always say, "Life is not fair." But we want it to be. That is why most people of our world are such devoted fans of the John Wayne "white hat" movies where the bad guys in the black hats get blown away while John Wayne and Maureen O'Hara smilingly walk into the sunset. That is also why we sometimes duck the truth when it is unpleasant. But, even then, there are times when we can't avoid the truth—and if we are not prepared for reality, the blow can be greater than it seems possible to bear.

No matter who you are; no matter what your station in life may be: *life is difficult*. We cannot escape problems— they go right along with us, walking in our footsteps.

That's why no solution is forever. As I've heard Norman Vincent Peale put it, "The only people without problems are in the cemetery."

Furthermore, it's in the way we meet problems that life has its meaning. In fact, that's what life is all about— solving life's problems. No life escapes problems. How happy we are depends on how successfully we solve our problems. Once we realize that, then we can quit blaming others. Because ultimately, we have to take responsibility for our own bitterness. How much energy is wasted by people who mentally replay their bitter disappointments, saying "It wasn't my fault," or "If only . . ."! Nursing a disappointment never resulted in its cure.

A second kind of person I counsel is the one who is *disillusioned*—one who has lost his or her dreams. In my home state of Oklahoma, the number of banks going under is amazing. In recent years, no less than fifty-six banking institutions have closed! And according to Governor Henry Bellmon, more than eighty others are in danger of going under. It's not only banks and businesses in Oklahoma, but all across America, companies which were once the picture of stability are now folding. And the impact on people's lives is devastating. The strain on one's marriage, children, and friendships is enormous. Many disillusioned people are having to start all over at a time in their lives when they dreamed they would have it made.

How difficult it is to live without our dreams! Some time back I heard that several nursing homes had decided to place video games in their lobbies. The rationale was that grandchildren would be enticed to come to the nursing homes to play video games. Just *maybe* they would stay to visit a few minutes with their grandmother or granddad. Think of the shattered dreams of these elderly people, to realize that their years of work and sacrifice merited less loyalty than Pac-Man. The result is a lot of bitterness and resentment. As I have said again and again, we may have a right to bitterness and resentment, but even if we do, can we afford the cost?

So then, what do we do with bitterness and resentment? In the preceding chapters I've tried to deal with some of the specific causes of bitterness. In the following pages, I want to offer six steps to help you deal with bitter experiences in general. These steps are applicable to any bitter experience:

1. Keep your attitude under control.

This will have to be a deliberate act because the *natural* thing to do is to lash out against injustice. That is not good stewardship of our time or our energy. Screaming out our pain may give a certain release, but the problems still remain. That's why it's important to underscore this truth: we may not have control over circumstances, but we can control our attitude towards those circumstances. In fact, the attitude with which we face life's circumstances is totally our own decision. When we know this, when we understand that life is not always fair, it enables us to refuse to get mired down in negative grumbling. The psalmist said, "I waited patiently for the Lord; and he inclined unto me, and heard my cry. He brought me up also out of a horrible pit, out of the miry clay, and set my feet upon a rock, and established my goings" (Psalm 40:1, 2).

One of the most inspiring verses in all the Bible is John 16:33. Jesus, in the Garden of Gethsemane, says, "Be of good cheer; I have overcome the world." Now on the surface of it that may not seem too fantastic, but look a little further. Jesus was facing whipping and humiliation, rejection by His disciples and the people of Israel; and worst of all, death on the cross as a common criminal. And yet, in the face of that, He said, "Be of good cheer; I have overcome the world." This tells me that Jesus knew the real battle was our attitude toward the events of life. The real struggle that we face is never external, but within. And Jesus won that battle, and we through His grace and strength can win it, too. We can take our attitude in our own control and determine to keep it open, accepting, and patient.

2. Reaffirm to yourself that bitterness and resentment are wrong for you.

The human race was made in the image of God. When you accepted Christ into your life, you restored that birthright. You reclaimed your heritage in God. Negative thinking is destructive to your divine image. Lashing out, grumbling in bitterness, and immersing your thoughts and conversation in anger only add to your unhappiness. And even though some people and certain events can trigger negative feelings in us, we have to be stronger than those situations. But it is up to us to enforce that faith attitude in our lives.

The truth is that certain people or situations can literally be a pain if we let them be. When that happens, a variety of distressing symptoms can follow. (That's where we get the phrases "He's a real pain in the neck" and "You make me sick.") But even though people can cause us genuine problems, the real enemy is the bitterness and resentment we take on.

Injustice destroys life as you want it to be. You cannot change this fact—so, accept it and turn your energies to exploring what can be done with what is left. This is the element that will make the difference in your future.

3. Forgive.

Jesus said in Matthew 5:23, 24: "Therefore if thou bring thy gift to the altar, and there rememberest that thy brother hath aught against thee; Leave there thy gift before the altar, and go thy way; first be reconciled to thy brother, and then come and offer thy gift."

If anyone ever had a right to bitterness, it was Jesus Christ as He was hanging on the cross. But even in His most painful moment, He rejected bitterness to set an example for us. His cure—and your cure for the wrongs against you—is simple: "Father, forgive them, for they know not what they do."

You may say that they know very well what they are doing, and that's why it's impossible for you to forgive them. The answer is still for you to forgive them, and to pray, "Father, forgive them." When you can say this, your heart has begun to heal. The highest level on which any of us can live is the level where we return good for evil. It is the highest level of spiritual and personal health.

4. Know that forgiveness always includes forgetting.

When the missionaries first came to Labrador, they found no word in the Eskimo language for forgiveness. They had to make up a new word, which in Eskimo meant, *"not being able to think about it anymore."* That's the critical message for us when we work at forgiving someone who has wronged us. We have to work on our attitude until we can truthfully say we are not able to think about it anymore. Forgiveness *must* mean forgetting.

One woman who visited me said that her hobby was tending her flower garden. She said, "You would be amazed at the number of disappointments I have buried in my garden." We may not have a garden, but we must find a way to bury our bitterness, to leave it there and to forget it.

Clara Barton had a wholesome attitude about disappointing experiences. When she was asked about a cruel thing that had been done to her, she replied, "I distinctly remember forgetting about that." She had not only forgiven, she had forgotten.

David Seabury said, "Experience shows that the pressure of undrained wounded emotion plays a great part in creating fatigue, nervousness and worry, even in youthful days." If bitterness is never put to rest, it stays to drain us, to limit us, to cripple us. And the best way to get rid of it is to forgive the cause and to forget it.

5. Remind yourself that you do not have any right to revenge.

Booker T. Washington once wrote, "No man shall ever narrow or degrade my soul by making me hate him." As anyone who lives in America knows, the inequities that black people have had to suffer have been terribly wrong. And yet, Washington, one of the great black Americans, recognized that hate would degrade him more than any of the degradations he had to undergo in white society. Though there may have been adequate cause for wanting revenge, he realized that it would ultimately hurt him more than what anyone else could do to him. In other words, he could not afford to seek revenge—it would "narrow and degrade" his soul.

Hebrews 12:14, 15 says, "Follow peace with all men, and holiness, without which no man shall see the Lord:

Looking diligently lest any man fail of the grace of God; lest any root of bitterness springing up trouble you, and thereby many be defiled." Any time there's bitterness, it affects not only you and your family, but also the people you work with, your relatives, people you come in contact with, and even your church. When bitterness creeps in, it defiles. When we seek revenge, we can never be satisfied. When we strive to get even, we can never know when we're even, because that bitter feeling is not erased through acts of revenge.

There is a story about a woman who was bitten by her dog. She was advised by her physician to write her last wishes, since she might succumb to rabies. She spent so much time with pencil and paper, the doctor finally asked just how long her will was going to be. "Will?" she snorted. "I'm writing a list of people I'm going to bite."

Is this your attitude? Do you want to bite back or heal? Do you want to hurt or help? You can't afford revenge. It will cost you more than it will cost anyone else.

6. Be constructive—rebuild what has been torn down.

In the quaint language of Lord Herbert, "He who cannot forgive others breaks the bridge over which he must pass himself." If we are unwilling to rebuild relationships with our enemies or our friends, then we break down the bridge between ourselves and God.

God's Word tells how to avoid bitterness before it begins: "Look after each other so that not one of you will fail to find God's best blessings" (Hebrews 12:15 TLB). What if we sought God's "best blessings" for a marriage partner, or a child or parent, or fellow worker? Could bitterness take root? You and I cannot pray with clenched

150

fists. The prayer Jesus taught His disciples has one soul-searching line, "Father, forgive us as we forgive. . . ." (*See* Luke 11:4.) When we pray to forgive others, we not only help ourselves, we build a bridge of reconciliation.

It has helped me to know that God will never be bitter toward me. Therefore, He is teaching me not to be bitter toward others. Can you accept His example, and know true peace of mind?

Which will you choose to be: *bitter?* or *better?* Will you choose to bend or break? If life has given you a lemon, will you choose to make lemonade, or emphasize the bitterness of the lemon? The decision is yours. I believe with all my heart that following these six steps when you face injustice will always bring you out on top. We're given that promise.

> *And now, dear friends of mine, I beg you not to be unduly alarmed at the fiery ordeals which come to test your faith, as though this were some abnormal experience. You should be glad, because it means that you are sharing in Christ's suffering. One day, when He shows Himself in full splendor, you will be filled with the most tremendous joy.*
>
> 1 Peter 4:12 PHILLIPS

LESSONS FROM THE TREES

Sprouts of renewed life

Trees reproduce themselves through seeds, nuts, and fruit after reaching maturity. When we look at a tree that is flourishing and fruitful, we see obvious signs of life and vitality. But if it is cut down, there is no green foliage, no fruit, no appearance of life. When we look at the dead stump, we see no indication that there may still be life in the roots. Many trees, when cut down or broken off, will propagate themselves by growing new sprouts from the living roots. These sprouts often become mature trees, once again bearing fruit.

This is what Job had in mind when he described his miserable condition:

> *For there is hope for a tree, if it is felled, that it will sprout again and that its shoots will flourish. Though its roots age in the earth and its stump dies in the ground, at the scent of water it will bud and branch out like a young plant. But when a man dies, he is laid prostrate; he expires, and where is he?*
>
> Job 14:7–10 MLB

Job's life had been cut down. He had lost all of his wealth, his family, and his health. He was reduced to a mere stump of what he had once been. And all his wife and best friends could tell him was that he probably deserved it!

God allowed Satan to cut Job down as far as possible— yet He made sure Job's life was spared (*see* Job 2:6). Job was cut down to the ground, but he wasn't uprooted! He still had life, and where there is life, there is hope. Yet in his misery and despair, Job believed he was as good as dead. His hope was uprooted (*see* Job 19:10) and he became absorbed in bitterness and self-pity. "If only I could live again!" he moaned (*see* Job 14:11–14). Job was only looking at the dead stump of his life and didn't consider that he could sprout again. But Job did sprout again—and thrive—as Job 42:10–17 reveals.

If you have been cut down, if you are bitter over losing everything meaningful in life, if you feel as good as dead—remember that you are still alive, and where there is life, there is hope. Don't give in to bitterness and self-pity. Don't nurse a grudge. Instead, follow the six steps I've outlined in this chapter, and trust that God will restore meaning and joy to your life.

Forgiveness:

Using an ancient remedy for inner healing

"He who cannot forgive others breaks the bridge over which he must pass himself."

GEORGE HERBERT

Bitterness is destructive; forgiveness is constructive. Bitterness gnaws at your insides; forgiveness calms your insides. Bitterness is human; forgiveness divine. Bitter experiences can become so pervasive that they determine who a person is. An angry person whose spouse has left him or her for another person can live his or her entire life bitterly protesting the injustice he or she has suffered. The parent whose child was killed by a drunk driver can spend the rest of his waking moments bitter at the stupidity and futility of what happened.

People can spend so much time being bitter, that they genuinely become "bitter persons." As the Bible says, "For as he thinketh in his heart, so is he" (Proverbs 23:7). As the bitterness becomes greater and greater, it can break you unless its cause is confronted, and its cure applied.

Don't misunderstand me; people have a right to be upset about injustices. The rapes, the abuse of children, the murders and robberies, and all the heinous crimes that plague our society cannot simply be swept under the rug. Yet, we must not allow bitterness to destroy us.

Maya Angelou, an American author, singer, and television producer, described this best. She once told a group of writers the injustices and discrimination she had experienced as a woman and a black. In the question and answer period afterwards, someone asked her, "How did you keep from being bitter and angry?"

She said, "Wait a minute. Bitterness and anger are two different things. I've never allowed myself to be bitter, but I've been plenty angry. Bitterness turns in upon you and eats away at your soul, whereas anger can cause you to work to change what's wrong. Bitterness, no; anger, yes!"

The best cure for bitterness is forgiveness. And you can claim the power of forgiveness in your own life by following these simple biblical steps:

1. Understand and acknowledge the weight of your bitterness.

One of the hardest things in the world is to pretend everything is fine when the whole world seems to be collapsing around you. In our competitive social and economic structures, we reward people who are able to suppress their emotions and we punish people who seemingly can't control theirs. And, certainly, there are times when it's inappropriate to express personal emotions. But denial of bitter disappointments can build up tensions inside which can break us if we don't address them. I've seen men whose businesses have gone under who were still pretending they were rich. They were unwilling to deal with their defeat. Sooner or later, that will leave them full of bitterness.

Jesus displayed anger, but never bitterness. In every situation which had the potential for bitterness, Jesus showed a spirit of love and forgiveness. He even forgave those who crucified Him. Out of the cross came a resurrection. That spirit of forgiveness is essential to overcoming bitter experiences.

2. Persist in your struggle to forgive the one who has wronged you.

Of all the challenges in life, none is more difficult than forgiving someone who has wronged you. Resentment keeps our insides festering; the inequities keep provoking us; and the smallest things trigger past pain. But we will only magnify our suffering if we don't offer full and complete forgiveness to those to whom we feel so bitter. And though it may take several tries before we're truly cleansed, we have to keep trying.

Winston Churchill experienced many failures and many successes in his lifetime. He was once asked what was the most important lesson he had learned in life. He spelled it out in seven words: "Never give up. Never, never give up."

That especially applies to extending forgiveness. We must never, never cease trying to forgive those who've wronged us, even though it may seem that all the wrong and blame is at their doorstep. We can't quit trying. When Jesus was asked how many times you should forgive a brother who has sinned against you, He replied, "Seventy times seven."

The reason Jesus chose "seventy times seven" was because the Jews believed the number seven was a perfect number. To forgive someone "seventy times seven" was the same as saying, "Keep forgiving them forever." Persist in your efforts to forgive someone—even if you have to forgive them the "seventy times seven" that Jesus talks about.

Sometimes, just when you think you've forgiven someone, bitterness may rear its ugly head and the old feelings of anger well up inside you. But, when it does, don't let it linger. Refuse to give it hospitality. Keep seeking the power of forgiveness. The peace that can come from true forgiveness will be worth every bit of the struggle. And if it seems impossible, remember that God has forgiven you "seventy times seven."

3. Forgive yourself.

One of the first steps to take in addressing the bitter experiences of life is to claim God's forgiveness for your life. A famous man once moaned, "I can pardon everyone's mistakes but my own."

There's nothing more destructive than being unable to forgive yourself for your mistakes. Yet it's so hard! Sometimes, it's difficult because we're the only ones who truly know how responsible we were for what happened. Inside we groan at the realization—if we had only done differently, if we had only been more willing to go the second mile, if we only had not said what we said. Over and over, the pain of our mistakes keeps haunting us.

God forgives you, and you can forgive yourself. You can conquer your own inability to forgive yourself. In the Book of Romans, Paul writes:

> We are more than conquerors through him
> who loved us. For I am sure that neither death,

> nor *life,* nor *angels,* nor *principalities,* nor
> *things present,* nor *things to come,* nor *powers,*
> nor *height,* nor *depth,* nor *anything else in all*
> *creation,* will *be able to separate us from the*
> *love of God in Christ Jesus our Lord.*
>
> *Romans 8:37–39* RSV

God's love is boundless; He wills for you to accept His divine forgiveness both from Him and yourself.

4. Claim the peace that comes from forgiveness.

When Leonardo da Vinci was working on his painting *The Last Supper,* he became angry with a certain man. Losing his temper, he lashed the other fellow with bitter words and threats. Returning to his canvas, he attempted to work on the face of Jesus, but was unable to do so. Finally, he put down his tools and sought out the man and asked his forgiveness. The man accepted his apology and da Vinci was able to return to his workshop and finish painting the face of Jesus.

What an inspiring story! Harboring anger and bitterness *will* deprive you of direction, of purpose, of power. But, when you let go of those feelings—when you truly forgive yourself or another—a sense of strength and purpose will settle over you and you will again be able to chart a new course for your life. Someone once said that, "Never does the human soul appear so strong as when it forgoes revenge and dares to forgive an injury."

Let go of your bitterness forever. When you do, you will find power in forgiveness! You will find peace in forgiveness! You will find strength in forgiveness!

One of the most courageous stories of forgiveness I've ever heard also involved one of the most brutal and savage of crimes. A young teenage girl, a popular and serious student, was driving home alone one night when it happened. Pausing at a stop sign, she had no time to escape when three men, all brothers, yanked open the doors of her car and told her to "Move over!" Numbed by drugs and alcohol, the men drove the girl to an isolated spot where they each raped her. Then, in a sudden moment of lucidity, they realized the seriousness of their crime and, without warning, one of the trio strangled the girl to death, thinking this would keep them from being caught.

Fortunately the men were arrested, but the trial was a long and bitter ordeal for the victim's family. The girl's mother seemed to suffer the most. Her eyes, filled with a mixture of pain and hate, followed the court proceedings as the three men were tried and found guilty. Her vacant expression rarely changed. Even at the moment of sentencing, there was no relief as she heard the three men sentenced to spend the rest of their lives in prison. All she could feel was hatred and bitterness. It consumed her life almost as if she personally had to hate them to avenge her daughter's murder.

As the months passed, she grew increasingly bitter and her pastor and friends became concerned about her well-being. She, too, began to realize that hatred and bitterness were destroying her, and she went to her pastor for help. One morning, in a counseling session, as they prayed, she cried out, "Oh, God, no one else on earth has more pain to bear than I do. How can I possibly forgive these men who have taken my daughter from me?"

That night, as the mother tossed and turned in her bed, she had a dream. In it, she became the mother of her daughter's murderers. And, in the dream, she was consumed with guilt, with pain and suffering, knowing that her sons had killed an innocent human being.

160

Jolted awake by the force of the dream, the mother opened her eyes wide, suddenly aware that somewhere out there a mother was suffering along with her. Her sons had cruelly and with malice decided to snap out the life of another. Her sorrow was double-edged. She had lost her sons, and she had to live with the pain that her sons were miserable failures.

At least, the girl's mother had lost a daughter whom everyone loved and respected. From that moment on, her bitterness and hatred changed to a more normal state of grief and sorrow, as she focused her attention on the process of healing, rather than on the festering sore of revenge. The healing power of forgiveness changed her life.

That's the possibility before you today as well. Forgiveness can be yours both to give and to receive. It can bring a new peace to your life.

5. Develop a habit of forgiving love.

Habits are funny things. Rightly developed, they help us do without thinking the things that need to be done. It's like brushing our teeth: when we get up in the morning, we don't debate whether or not we should brush our teeth; we just do it: it's become a habit.

One of the Christian's goals should be to develop the *habit* of forgiving others. In other words, develop such a life-style in Christ that we never debate whether to forgive or not: we simply do it because it's become the way we are—it's become a habit. I don't know if I'll ever develop this habit as much as I need to, but I do know that there have been some extraordinary Christians who have been able to do it.

One of the most remarkable that I've ever read about was Father Kolby, a priest who was interned in the

German concentration camp at Auschwitz during World War II. During his internment, it was a common practice that whenever anyone escaped, the remaining prisoners would be severely punished. The diabolical method was to gather the prisoners together and then choose fourteen of them to be placed in a cell where the rest could see them. They were then starved to death. Most of those placed in the cell would not last more than a few days due to their already precarious health. The maximum endurance was seldom more than seven or eight days. It was not only punishment for breaking the rules, but it also deterred prisoners from helping anyone escape in the future because the cost in suffering to those left behind was too high.

One day it was discovered that a prisoner had escaped, so all the camp prisoners were herded together. The guards began naming the fourteen prisoners who were to pay the price for this latest escape. When they called one man's name, he began screaming and crying, begging to be allowed to live. He had a family, a wife and children, and he desperately wanted to survive.

That's when Father Kolby stepped forward and volunteered to take the man's place. The Germans permitted it. They then placed the prisoners, including Father Kolby, in the cell to die. A young man talked with Father Kolby and said he would always hate the Germans for what they had done. Father Kolby's response was, "We must love, not hate." *He was forgiving some of the cruelest behavior known to man!*

Life for the condemned men began to pass. As usual, most died within days. When only four remained, the Nazis decided it had gone on long enough and ordered the prisoners injected with carbolic acid.

What an example of forgiving love! Father Kolby didn't learn it on the spot. As his story relates, it was a habit he had practiced. Though I hope none of us will ever have to make that kind of sacrifice, still the principle is one we need to follow, namely, to practice the habit of forgiving love. When we do, we will discover how full and rich our lives can become. We will become like the legendary phoenix, which the ancient Egyptians believed was a bird consumed by fire, that rose up from its own ashes and assumed a new life. That can apply to our lives as well. Once forgiveness has rooted out our bitterness, we too, can rise up a new creature in Christ Jesus. From the ashes of bitterness, we can forgive and be forgiven.

LESSONS FROM THE TREES

Roots

Nothing is more critical to a tree than its roots. Though the visible part of a tree may be relatively small, it may have a root system that runs on endlessly. Some large spreading oak trees, for example, have root systems that measure *hundreds of miles!*

To many, the most important part of the tree is its visible part, the limbs and leaves. But without the support of a strong root system, it would perish. That's why a tall tree can withstand the constant buffeting of high winds and storms: its roots provide a strong anchor.

In the same way, deep spiritual roots anchor us against the unexpected. We cannot withstand the storms of life without a healthy root system. Bitterness can destroy our roots like a disease. That's why there's nothing more important to our spiritual roots than ridding our lives of bitterness. Forgiving those who have wronged us, and learning to forgive ourselves, will keep our roots healthy. It opens us up to the power that comes from daily prayer, daily reading of the Bible, and regular attendance at the House of the Lord.

The prophet Jeremiah wrote:

> *Blessed is the man who trusts in the Lord and whose confidence is the Lord. He is like a tree planted by water, that sends out its roots by the stream, and it does not fear when heat comes, for its leaves remain green; in the year of drought it is not anxious, for it does not fail to yield fruit.*

Jeremiah 17:7 8, MLB

Like well-watered roots, our trust in God will keep us green and fruitful. If we keep ourselves well-rooted in Christ, we won't become bitter when we face scorching heat or times of drought. Instead, if we can learn to forgive, our spiritual roots will grow strong. This gives us a firm anchor so that when the winds of life whip us around, we can *bend and not break.*

Giving Thanks:

Tapping the mysterious power of thankfulness

"My God, I have never thanked Thee for my thorn [blindness]. I have thanked Thee a thousand times for my roses, but never once for my thorn. I have been looking forward to a world where I shall get compensation for my cross as itself a present glory. Teach me the glory of my cross; teach me the value of my thorn. Show me that I have climbed to Thee by the path of pain. Show me that my tears have been my rainbow."

GEORGE MATHESON

One of the most challenging verses in the entire New Testament is this: "In every thing give thanks: for this is the will of God in Christ Jesus concerning you" (1 Thessalonians 5:18). I knew it for sure when a special friend of this ministry recently asked me, "How can you give thanks for cancer?"

I said, "Pardon me, Will?"

He said, "The Bible says, 'In every thing give thanks'; how do you give thanks for cancer?"

Not only did his question shock me, but I had no idea he had cancer. When I asked him about it, this is what he told me:

I began to notice that I was feeling tired and lacking energy, but I thought maybe it was just lack of sleep or my age. I kept on pushing even though I was constantly dragging. Then I realized that when I stood up, I would be dizzy. I'd stand still a little while and it would go away. You know, everyone has had a little bit of that at sometime or other; mine had always gone away before and I was sure it would this time as well. Gradually, though, the dizziness increased until it was too serious to ignore.

Though it was just a month until time for my annual physical, my wife went with me to the hospital. Naturally, one of the things they did was to take a blood test. The results showed severe anemia. A few days later, I went back in for additional tests and the report this time knocked me off my feet. I had leukemia: cancer of the blood. I couldn't believe it. I hadn't done anything different than I had been doing all my life. My physical the year before had shown me to be in excellent health.

And the irony of it all was that just the week before my wife and I had decided to sell our business and take some time off to enjoy life a little more. We hadn't had a real vacation in thirty years.

When he paused, his eyes misted up and his voice cracked, "We're going to sell the business all right, but not so we can take some time off."

Now I knew more what we meant when he asked, "How do you give thanks for cancer?" That's not an easy question in the abstract; it's especially difficult when you're face-to-face with a friend and a victim. As I put my hand on his shoulder, I tried to enter into the arena of his life and understand how terrible this situation must be for him. On the outside he looked the picture of health, but inside a malignancy was eating away at him. It seemed very improbable that he and his wife would get to enjoy as many of the benefits of all their years of hard work as they had hoped. Plus, he was facing a future of uncertainty, painful therapy, and treatment. How could he be thankful for that? Why *should* he be, anyway? Why should anyone be thankful for something so awful? What possibly could the Bible mean with its orders to be thankful for everything, what I call its *Thankfulness Imperative?* To help us better understand 1 Thessalonians 5:18, notice how other translations render that same verse:

> *Always be thankful no matter what happens, for that is God's will for you to belong to Christ Jesus.*
>
> LIVING LETTERS

> *Be thankful, whatever the circumstances may be. If you follow this advice you will be working out the will of God expressed to you in Christ Jesus.*
>
> PHILLIPS

> *Give thanks whatever happens; for this is what God in Christ wills for you.*
>
> NEB

What does it mean to give thanks in the midst of the unexpected, the tragic, the life-threatening?

Recently, I purchased a small booklet entitled *Comfort for Troubled Christians,* by J. C. Brumfield. One section is entitled, "What Is Happiness?" That's a question that I'm constantly being asked, so I thumbed to it immediately. I was fascinated by Brumfield's answer. He listed several examples of unhappy people whom he had encountered; each of them had identified what they felt would make them happy:

> First, there was a lady in the hospital who was desperately ill. She had been sick a long time and her progress seemed especially slow. She was gradually getting worse, not better. She said, "If I could be well again, I would be the happiest woman in the world." That was her idea of happiness, and it wasn't too hard to know where she was coming from. Until you've lain on your back for weeks, maybe even months . . . until you've suffered constant pain and physical failure . . . until you've had your body fail you, you really don't know how precious health is. So when someone says having their health again would make them happy, it's not a casual statement. Health is a great gift from God.

But each of us knows many healthy people who are not happy. In fact, there are invalids who are happier than some healthy people. The strongest, best-looking, healthiest persons can be eaten up on the inside with unhappiness. Physical well-being in and of itself does not make for happiness.

> Then there was a blind woman who had undergone surgery on her eyes. In the process of determining the success of the operation, the doctor slowly unwound the bandages. As the suspense mounted, the woman exclaimed, "If I can just see, I will be happy." Sight is such a precious thing that it's easy to understand what she meant. The beauty of the universe, the

warmth of a smile, the joy of watching children play are all dependent upon vision and sight. Without it, an important part of existence is lost.

Yet, is physical sight the foundation for happiness? You and I know people who have perfectly good eyesight, but profess that life is terrible for them; some become so desperate they even take their lives. And yet they can see; they have perfectly great vision. Great eyesight does not by itself make for happiness, either.

In another case, a crippled boy lay on his bed in the orthopedic ward of a hospital in Lincoln, Nebraska. As his parents sat with him, he looked wistfully out the window at other children playing in the street and said, "If I could just walk, I'd be the happiest boy in the world." For a crippled boy, it's not hard to understand why he felt the way he did about walking. Never to be able to run nor navigate without crutches or a wheelchair is an awful loss, especially for a young boy, with all the energy and enthusiasm for life which he has.

But how many people do you know who can both run and walk and yet are not happy? In fact, the vast majority of the people on the face of the earth can walk. Yet, does that ability make them happy? Does the mere fact that they can get up and go whenever they wish provide the secret of happiness? We know it doesn't.

Then there was the man who had lost his job after 18 years with the same company. His modest savings account had vanished quickly; bills began mounting up; creditors began calling. His family began to be in want. As he stated his problem, he said, "If I just had a little

money, not a lot, just enough for the necessities
of life, I'd be happy." And until you've faced
the day not knowing where your next meal is
coming from, you really can't understand this
need.

Because of our ministry at Feed the Children, I've not
only seen thousands who were hungry, I have seen them
literally starve to death and was not able to stop it. I've
seen men who once had been strong and healthy, with
families and possessions, reduced to skin and bones—
mere shadows of what they had been previously.

Being without the necessities of life is terrible. And in
our bountiful nation and world, it should never happen.
Yet, is having these necessities the secret to happiness?
How many people do you know who are terribly discon-
tent with their status and station in life? They feel terribly
deprived because they don't have enough things. And
what about some rich people who have more money than
they could ever spend? Some of them are among the most
miserable people on earth! They have everything and feel
they should be happy; but when they aren't, it eats them
alive. They're never satisfied with what they have. As one
friend of mine put it, "They don't know when the sun is
shining." It's often been said and constantly demon-
strated that money is not the secret of happiness.

A single woman said, "If I just had a husband,
I'd be happy." This is a feeling that more people
are confronting as divorce rates soar. For many
the prospect of living alone and growing old
alone is terribly depressing. The words of God
to Adam were, "It is not good that man should
be alone." And that applies to men and women
today as well. Aloneness can become corrosive;
it can become isolation; it can cause small

*events to be magnified far out of proportion.
And left unaddressed, isolation can do serious
damage to one's emotional well-being.*

But is a spouse the secret of happiness? There are thousands of men and women who are married but seem to think that if they could get out of their marriages, it would be the happiest day of their lives. Marriage isn't the answer to happiness.

Yet, the verse written by Paul to the Thessalonians admonishes us to thank God in everything, no matter what the circumstances may be. This is one of the *hard sayings* of the Bible. How can we thank God for *every* circumstance we encounter? How can we thank God for sickness, the death of a loved one, loneliness, and other misfortunes that may come our way? How can a sick woman in a hospital be thankful for illness, a blind person for being blind, a cripple for not being able to walk, an unemployed person for being out of a job, a single person for being alone?

The more I thought about these questions, the more I realized there was one repetitive theme throughout each of them: *they identified happiness with possessing one important thing they didn't have.* No matter what else they had, lacking that one thing made them unhappy. What they didn't have took away from what they had. In other words, because of the one negative in their life, all of the rest of life was negative as well.

Now let me say that I'm not treating casually sickness, bankruptcy, blindness, aloneness, or any of the multitude of bad things that can happen to us. Rather, I'm suggesting that one of the reasons they are so bad is because of what they do to the rest of our lives and relationships. All of the other important dimensions to our existence become tainted and diminished because of the negative that has

171

invaded our life stream and poisoned our attitude. The one bad apple destroys the entire bushel of good apples.

Most of us have had situations in which we discover too late the truth of Orson Welles' statement: "The worst thing in life is not getting what you want; the next worst thing is getting what you want." Too many times we get what we want and then find out that it did not bring the happiness we were so certain would ensue.

Of course, the classic case in literature of a person wanting what he did not have is the fable of King Midas. He was unhappy that he did not have more gold and asked the gods to grant his wish that everything he touched would turn to gold. They did. When he touched a beautiful flower, its hues and colors all turned to gold. When he kissed his daughter, the apple of his eye, she turned to a statue of gold. And so on it went: everything he treasured in its natural state became gold. Finally, in desperation, he petitioned the gods to reverse his wish. And in so doing he realized how inappropriate his wish for gold had been. The one thing he had wanted, instead of bringing happiness, had brought great sadness.

Robert Service, in his poem "The Spell of the Yukon," written during his time in Alaska, made the same point:

> *I wanted the gold and I sought it;*
> *I scrabbled and mucked like a slave.*
> *Was it famine or scurvy—I fought it;*
> *I hurled my youth into a grave.*
>
> *I wanted the gold and I got it—*
> *Came out with a fortune last fall—*
> *Yet somehow life's not what I thought it,*
> *And somehow the gold isn't all.*

But the thrust of the Bible's Thankfulness Imperative is not simply to say we're unhappy because we want too much. It's saying that in the midst of everything that's happening to us, we have to find a way to be thankful. The corrective for having a terrible attitude about all of life is to be thankful even for the negative, for the one thing you wish you didn't have. The Bible is not saying, "Everything that happens to us in life is great and wonderful." Rather, it's offering a fundamental insight into life and happiness that's valid even when something terrible happens to us.

Matthew Henry, the famous scholar, was once robbed by thieves. Afterwards, he wrote these words in his diary: "Let me be thankful first, because I was never robbed before; second, because although they took my purse, they did not take my life; third, because, although they took my all, it was not much; and fourth, because it was I who was robbed, not I who robbed." He knew what it meant to be thankful in everything.

Let us look on the other side of the coin and ask the question, "Are we thankful for the good times and the good things of life when we have them?" Dr. Scott Peck, in his runaway best-seller, *The Road Less Traveled*, wrote that the amazing miracle of modern medicine is not the number of people cured of some serious illness; rather, the real miracle is how many people are not sick to begin with.

How many people go through terrible emotional trauma and come out without permanent impairment? How many people are exposed to the worst kinds of disease and resist contracting it? How many people experience life-threatening situations and escape unscathed? That's the truly amazing thing about life, that so much good happens to us. And certainly, it would be appropriate to ask, "Do I thank God when I'm not sick, or for all the times when I had my loved ones, or for when I wasn't lonely, or when I find myself not facing trials?'' Thankfulness is a full-time job—not a part-time one.

George Matheson, the famous blind preacher of Scotland, once said, "My God, I have never thanked Thee for my thorn [blindness]. I have thanked Thee a thousand times for my roses, but never once for my thorn. I have been looking forward to a world where I shall get compensation for my cross as itself a present glory. Teach me the glory of my cross; teach me the value of my thorn. Show me that I have climbed to Thee by the path of pain. Show me that my tears have made my rainbow."

That's our challenge: to see every situation as having its redemptive possibilities—every tear as ultimately producing a rainbow. The twentieth century life-style challenges us to purchase more and more, but the Bible teaches us to stop and be thankful for what we have, and not merely for the material benefits of life, but also for the things that have caused us to suffer, to cry, and to be sad. We would not enjoy the beauty of the sunrise had it not been for the blackness of the night.

One of the greatest joys that I have experienced while in the ministry is visiting the sick in the hospital. It is always a joy to see the power of God begin its work in the lives of hospital patients. This power always seems to work *inside* before it works *outside*. One of the blessings I identified when I was seriously ill was that when I was lying on my back, I was more prone to *look up* to God!

All of these experiences prepared me for my interaction with my friend Will, whom I mentioned at the beginning of this chapter. I said to him, "Will, I agree that cancer is nothing to be thankful for. But in the midst of this, there are a lot of things about your having cancer I am thankful for: I'm thankful you have a precious wife to go through this experience with you. I'm thankful you can have great doctors and a super hospital to treat you. I'm thankful for all the work and research that's going on to cure leukemia; in fact, many people are surviving who never used to have a chance. I'm thankful that you're a Christian and know the meaning of prayer. And I'm glad you found out about your cancer as early as you did. Those are just a few of the things I'm thankful for in your case, Will. And I believe that's what Paul meant: not to be thankful for the bad thing itself, but to find some dimension of it that we can be thankful for. And in that way keep a victorious spirit over that which would try to destroy us."

Our example is always Christ. Everything that Jesus did was turned against Him. His friends forsook Him. He had no home. His work seemed in vain. And He was betrayed by one of His closest associates. Yet, He remained constant and committed to the task which lay before Him.

In whatever circumstance you find yourself, you, too, are challenged by Christ to be constant and committed; to be thankful. Here are some ways to do that:

1. Make a list of the persons for whom you should be thankful.

Conduct a *Thankfulness Inventory*. Start first in thankfulness for the three anchors of your faith. The first is God's Word: Psalm 119:130 says, "The entrance of thy words giveth light; it giveth understanding unto the simple." The second is the assurance that God loves you. The third is that God gave Christ for you. John 3:16 says it all, "For God so loved the world, that he gave his only begotten Son, that whosoever believeth in him should not perish, but have everlasting life."

8

Next, list the people who have been especially helpful to you. Marcus Aurelius, the great Roman emperor of the second century, compiled a series of meditations and thoughts during his latter years. But before he wrote anything, the very first of his twelve books names all the persons for whom he was thankful and what their contributions had meant to his life. As he sat in his tent on some distant battlefield, far from home and his family, he carefully identified the many persons who had given to him. How many people have contributed to your life? Have you thanked God for them?

Several years ago, I heard a sermon by a minister in Texas. He told how God had ministered to him from the book of Job at a time of especially difficult circumstances. His wife had cancer and the complications arising from that had taken their toll on their family, the church, and his work. As he read Job, the question kept racing through his mind, "How can I have any hope when there are no answers?" As he read, he discovered that God always answered Job with questions: "Were you there when I created the dawn? Were you there when I made the eagle soar into the sky?" (See Job 38:12 and 39:27.) The answers reflected the greatness of God. Through his own questions, this minister began to understand the answer for his situation.

That didn't seem especially revolutionary, but somehow it stuck with me. Two weeks later, I was in the same situation as the pastor I'd heard. Suddenly, it did begin to make sense. My questions to God became God's questions to me. Through living the questions, I began to find the answers. But I never let that pastor know how helpful he had been . . . until recently, that is. I sat down and wrote him a note and letter of appreciation for his help.

2. Make a list of all the things you have to be thankful for.

Are you always aware of when the sun is shining? How many good things do you have going for you that you've taken for granted? Remember the man who complained because he had no shoes, until he met a man who had no feet? We can be thankful that this principle of giving thanks puts us on a positive path even though we may be going through a very trying situation. Are we thankful that we can change our attitude this moment? We may be knocked down, but we're not knocked out!

3. Identify all of the negatives in your life that pull you down.

Once you've listed the negatives, then find something positive about each situation for which you can be thankful. I was stunned by the insight of Matthew Henry when he said he was thankful that he was the one who was robbed rather than being the robber. How terrible to carry around the guilt of having robbed another person!

Recently, a woman's husband had to have his leg amputated. When someone asked how her husband was taking it, she said, "He says he's thankful they're only taking one leg and not both!"

4. Restate the Scripture verse 1 Thessalonians 5:18 so that it becomes your personal life statement.

Too many times we read Scripture, but we don't appropriate it into our lives. But this verse deserves better. Try letting it become *your* verse, personally appropriated for all of your life:

*I will give thanks in all things! I know this is
God's will for my life now in this moment.*

Someone said that one dimension of original sin is
laziness. We Christians have to fight that as well. The
blessings of life don't just shower down upon us all the
time; sometimes, we have to take steps to make things
happen. Giving thanks is one such step. It requires an act
of will.

5. Be glad for the opportunities of this day.

One of my favorite Scripture verses is, "This is the day
which the Lord has made; let us rejoice and be glad in it"
(Psalm 118:24 RSV). Every day is a day that God has made
for you. It's a time when you can be glad for what has
come your way. A popular saying of several years back
was, "Today is the first day of the rest of your life." I've
found that very helpful. This is a new day we're facing.
More than that, it's a day that God has made for us. What
more could we want than a new start in God's time, to be
thankful, to rejoice, and to be glad? In all things, give
thanks!

6. Know that Jesus is Lord over all.

In the midst of trying situations, one of the things that
has helped me most is knowing who is truly Lord of life.
I read one time about a man who had this motto on his
office wall: "The answer when found will be simple." Dr.
E. Stanley Jones wrote about it and said, "The answer
always is. But of all the reductions from complexity to
simplicity, the greatest and profoundest is the early
Christian creed: *Jesus is Lord.*"

What has helped me the most, whether I face robbery,

loss of staff, or sickness, is to know that "All things work together for good to them that love the Lord and are called according to his purpose." As Joseph said to his brethren after they had sold him into slavery, "You meant evil against me; but God meant it for good." (*See* Genesis 50:20.)

Afterword: Robbed!
An unexpected opportunity to practice thankfulness

Ialways appreciate the personal testimonies of persons who have gone through some difficult experience. And although I'm glad for their testimony and I admire their courage and strength, I am usually secretly grateful that it was *their* experience and not *mine*. I know that God does not require me to experience everything I preach about, yet sometimes preachers get an opportunity to practice what they preach.

I had hardly finished the preceding chapter on thankfulness than the opportunity came for me to see how helpful its insights were. It was a Monday morning, the first of December. For our ministry, Monday is the most important day of the week; the first Monday of the month is especially important; and December, because of its being Christmas, is the most significant month of the year for Feed the Children. More people write to get involved in our ministry to children at that time of the year than at any other. I know that; my employees know that; and someone else did as well. As one of our trusted employees was returning from the Post Office in rush hour traffic, he was bumped from behind. He pulled over to see if there was any damage. When he did, three men in the other car climbed out of their car as well. As they were examining the damage, he suddenly felt a gun in his back and he was led to the ditch near the side of the road and forced to lie down with his face to the ground. All of this in broad daylight, on a busy interstate highway, in morning rush hour traffic!

Within minutes, his car and the mail for Feed the Children were gone. When he reported the matter to us and the police, we were dumbfounded. The mail and the gifts from some very special and precious people were gone.

A little while later, as I reflected on it, I remembered the response of Matthew Henry to being robbed, which I had written about in the preceding chapter. Let me quote it again:

> *Matthew Henry, the famous scholar, was once robbed by thieves. Afterwards, he wrote these words in his diary: "Let me be thankful first, because I was never robbed before; second, because although they took my purse, they did not take my life; third, because, although they took my all, it was not much; and fourth, because it was I who was robbed, not I who robbed." He knew what it meant to be thankful in everything.*

As I reread that, a strange feeling came over me. It was as if God had given me that story from the past to help me understand my present. As I thought more about it, I realized that I had some things to be thankful for, just like Matthew Henry.

First, I was thankful that I had never been robbed before. There have been many times both in America and overseas, that I have transported funds for the work of the ministry. But never had I been robbed before.

Second, even though they robbed us, they didn't physically hurt anyone. I was deeply thankful for that!

Third, even though they took everything—checks, letters, and cards—we will survive it.

And fourth—this was the most important—I'm thankful, as Matthew Henry put it, "because it was I who was robbed, and not I who robbed."

The next day after the robbery I met with our employees for chapel. I told them the details of the robbery and then described some of the things that had been going on inside me. I also shared with them some of the material from the preceding chapter of this book. I told them that this was another situation in which we needed to *bend, and not break.*

If the Bible is true, and I know it is, then this was clearly one of those times that we needed to be able to give thanks, regardless of the situation. I couldn't preach one thing and practice another. So we prayed for our robbers, that God would somehow reach them and that they would come to know Christ. I asked God for our anger and frustration to be removed, and not to let this adversely affect our work for Him that day or any of the days in the future.

The Apostle James wrote, "My brethren, count it all joy when ye fall into divers temptations" (James 1:2). Though it was difficult, in my heart I had to say to God, "Thank You, Lord, for this opportunity to be Your witness." I'm hopeful that whatever the future holds, I can do it with faith and hope and trust.

Every day we are writing our "Future Diary." Every act we take determines some dimension of the future. We can't face the future with bitterness. We can't face it with unforgiven resentment. Instead, we have to face it in the confidence that no matter what happens, "All things work together for good to them that love the Lord." That confidence enables me to put my trust in Him for all the tomorrows, knowing that He is the One who has the whole world in His hand, including my future and everyone else's as well.

Although I don't want to experience all the difficult things I've written about in this book, I am glad that in this instance what I had written worked for me. I'm sure the same will be true for you as you learn how to *bend without breaking.*

Dear Reader,

I'm genuinely honored that you have read this book. I hope it helps to meet a need that you have. That was certainly the intent I had in writing it. And if you have friends you feel could benefit from reading it, I hope you will give them a copy as well. We need all the help we can get, don't we?!

In fact, since I started working on this book, it's amazing the number of people who have told me how much they needed and wanted a book like this. As I've listened to them, I've had confirmed time and again how many people are trying hard to keep from breaking in the midst of some terribly difficult circumstances.

That's why I've included this brief note here in the back of the book. As you've read this book, perhaps there was some particular part of it that you found especially helpful in making it through a difficult time.

I would greatly appreciate it if you would share your

story with me. It's quite possible it would make the difference for some other person going through a similar circumstance.

As others respond, we can begin to build a repository of friends who have been able to bend and not break. Together, we can share our insights and helps through letters, newsletters, and even on television.

I'm greatly excited at the possibilities and I would welcome an opportunity to count you among this select group of caring persons. Please send me your story at the following address:

> Larry Jones
> BEND, DON'T BREAK
> P.O. Box 36
> Oklahoma City, OK 73101

Thanks so much for this opportunity to enable you to be of help to others. I look forward to hearing from you and to reading your personal prescription for *how to bend and not break.*